THE NATIONAL INSTITUTE OF
ECONOMIC AND SOCIAL RESEARCH

Occasional Papers
XXXVIII

PROFITS AND STABILITY OF MONOPOLY

2 DEAN TRENCH STREET, SMITH SQUARE, LONDON, SWIP 3HE

The National Institute of Economic and Social Research is an independent, non-profit-making body, founded in 1938. It has as its aim the promotion of realistic research, particularly in the field of economics. It conducts research by its own research staff and in cooperation with the universities and other academic bodies. The results of the work done under the Institute's auspices are published in several series, and a list of its publications will be found at the end of this volume.

PROFITS AND STABILITY OF MONOPOLY

M. A. UTTON

The right of the University of Cambridge to print and sell all manner of books was granted by Henry VIII in 1534. The University has printed and published continuously since 1584.

CAMBRIDGE UNIVERSITY PRESS

CAMBRIDGE
LONDON NEW YORK NEW ROCHELLE
MELBOURNE SYDNEY

Published by the Press Syndicate of the University of Cambridge
The Pitt Building, Trumpington Street, Cambridge CB2 1RP
32 East 57th Street, New York, NY 10022, USA
10 Stamford Road, Oakleigh, Melbourne 3166, Australia

First published 1986

Printed in Great Britain by the University Press, Cambridge

British Library cataloguing in publication data

Utton, M. A.
Profits and stability of monopoly. – (Occasional papers/The National Institute of Economic and Social Research; 38)
1. Monopolies 2. Profit 3. Stocks
I. Title II. Series
338.8′2 HD2757.2

Library of Congress cataloguing in publication data

Utton, M. A. (Michael A.), 1939–
Profits and stability of monopoly.
Bibliography.
Includes index.
1. Oligopolies. 2. Profit 3. Oligopolies–Great Britain
4. Profit–Great Britain I. Title
HD2757.3.U88 1986 338.8′2′0941 86–4226

ISBN 0 521 32550 1

CONTENTS

TABLES

PREFACE

A central question in industrial economics is the extent to which dominance in a particular market allows a firm to maintain abnormally high profits without gradually ceding its position to rivals. There is not only considerable controversy about the source of such profits – some contending that they rest on efficiency and others arguing equally strongly that they depend on market power – but also on the durability of large market shares over time.

Research on these issues in the United Kingdom has been hampered by the lack of systematic data on market shares and profitability. However, for many years, the Monopolies and Mergers Commission has been publishing detailed studies of the more concentrated sectors of British industry at the rate of about five or six per year. The reports usually contain the kind of information required for examining questions concerning market shares and profitability. The data used in this study have therefore been drawn largely from these reports, supplemented in a number of instances by similar information from the Price Commission. Given this data source the analysis is naturally confined to heavily concentrated markets where profitability is likely to be at its highest. In view, however, of the current policy of privatising intact previously state-owned monopolies, the performance of firms in such markets is likely to remain important for some time.

The project was assisted by a grant from the Office of Fair Trading and I would like to thank Malcolm Bradbury, Alan Bell, Graham Atkinson and Michael Doig for their continued support and encouragement. Once again it is a pleasure to record my gratitude to Sig Prais and Peter Hart for their many helpful and stimulating suggestions. Both the Director, Andrew Britton and the Secretary, Kit Jones gave me every encouragement during the course of the study. Successive drafts were typed with great efficiency by Susie John and the computations were carried out by Pam Watts and Diane Swan with their customary skill. The final draft was very ably prepared for the printer by Frances Robinson who also compiled the index.

It is hardly necessary to add that the Office of Fair Trading is in no way responsible for any of the views or interpretations expressed in the study. Together with any errors and shortcomings these are entirely my responsibility.

National Institute of Economic and Social Research
September 1985

M. A. UTTON

INTRODUCTION

THE ANALYSIS OF MARKET SHARES

A convenient starting point for the analysis of market shares in oligopoly is the theory of market prices associated with the Austrian school of economics, which has recently enjoyed a revival of interest.[1] In this approach great stress is placed on competition as a dynamic process, taking place amidst uncertainty and change. It is contrasted with the neo-classical theory of competition with its emphasis on equilibrium, and its comparative static method. The difference between the two theories is perhaps at its greatest in the treatment of monopoly. For writers of the Austrian school monopoly positions are won as a result of perceiving and acting upon opportunities for meeting a need in a way superior to existing methods, spurred on by the lure of profit. The high profits earned by monopolists, however, are, almost without exception, vulnerable to the innovating efforts of others seizing new opportunities. On this view, even if an existing monopolist seeks to maintain its market share by a variety of restrictive conditions or the purchase of any rivals, its position will ultimately be undermined by others.[2] Thus if, at a particular time, a number of monopoly market shares are observed across different industries, this is only to be expected from the competitive process. Subsequently these shares will decline, as others encroach on the monopoly or the 'market' itself may decline along with the profitability of the firms supplying it as other, more highly valued, substitutes take its place. A conclusion of the theory, therefore, is that firms dominant in a particular market will, over time, have to concede that dominance to others. They may be able to slow down the process by a series of exclusionary tactics and mergers but ultimately the strength of competition will prevail.

If this process is working actively, therefore, we should observe the decline over time of the market shares of the leading firms. From an empirical point of view the problem with this theory is the time period involved. The rate at which dominant positions are eroded may be expected to vary from industry to industry according to the types of technology involved and the stage of development reached (the process is likely to be slower in 'mature' industries, for example). But we get very little help from the theory as to whether a position of dominance will be eroded within five years or fifty.

The criticism has less force when used against those attempts to predict the market share of dominant firms using a comparative static analysis. The well-known dominant firm price leadership model, like the Austrian approach, also predicts the erosion in most cases of the market share of the dominant firm. In the simplest case the dominant firm is assumed to be the price maker which adjusts its price and output according to what it knows will be the joint supply of fringe firms which are assumed to have only a small fraction of the market. The higher the price, the greater the supply from the fringe (all of whom are assumed to behave like price takers) and the smaller the output of the dominant firm. For our purposes the interesting point is the following: unless the fringe firms simply break even at the dominant firm's price, both they and new entrants will be encouraged to increase their market shares at the expense of the dominant firm. The analysis, therefore, predicts a declining market share for the dominant firm, unless it is fortunate enough to be able to set a profit maximising price which leaves fringe firms with only a normal return, thus providing no incentive for their expansion or for new entry. Worcester (1957) develops this analysis in a number of ways but in particular he emphasises that so long as the dominant firm continues to shoulder the burden of price determination and passive output restriction to accommodate the fringe suppliers, its market share will dwindle even though there may be increasing returns to scale. In this case if, at the dominant firm's optimum price, fringe firms can earn a normal return,[3] then they will have a strong incentive to expand their output and thereby reduce costs. Similarly, entry will be attracted by the abnormal returns earned by the dominant firm. Thus, even in the case where the dominant firm has a cost advantage, its market share will be eroded while it remains the price leader.

It was the passive role assumed throughout this analysis that led Worcester and others to argue that in most instances the dominant firm price leadership model was essentially short-run. Sooner or later the dominant firm would respond actively to the erosion of its market share so that the structure of the market would evolve either into more evenly balanced oligopoly or monopoly. If the response of the dominant firm is unsuccessful or mistimed, something approaching a competitive structure might result, at least in cases of decreasing or constant returns to scale. To prevent the erosion of their market share dominant firms may engage periodically in aggressive policies of acquisition or by erecting entry barriers (by increased product differentiation for example) and so abandoning the price leadership role (Worcester, 1957, p. 342). Where a dominant market share has been maintained for some time, therefore, unless it depends crucially on a key patent it is likely to be due to an active merger policy.[4]

Since the contribution by Worcester, a great deal more attention has been given to the possibility that a dominant firm may forestall or at least delay the erosion of its market position by limit pricing. Much of the analysis has been concerned with the conditions under which a dominant firm (or group acting collusively) will be able and willing to set prices below the short-run profit maximising level by an amount just sufficient to prevent the entry of new firms.[5] For a time existing firms may be able to prevent entry by a limit price strategy but complete control may become increasingly difficult, partly in the group case by inter-firm competition, and partly by the erosion of the entry barrier by new methods, processes or products available to potential entrants. At various points, therefore, the limit price strategy may have to be modified either in an attempt to continue to prevent entry or at least to control the rate at which entry occurs. The progress from a limit price to a competitive price will depend on a number of factors some of which may be expected to vary from industry to industry: for example, the rate of innovation and technical change, the size of the existing group's current profits and their rate of discount and the rate at which it is technically possible for entry to occur.

The broad conclusion, however, is that unless entry is completely blockaded, we might expect market shares to be gradually eroded. A further exception should also be noted. Where a dominant firm has a significant cost or other advantage, but where nevertheless a significant competitive fringe also exists it may be in the interests of the dominant firm initially to set prices below either the fringe firms' unit costs or even its own in order to improve its market share by driving fringe firms out. Although this case is often quoted as a theoretical possibility and has recently been considerably refined it seems rather implausible for a number of reasons. First, it is not clear why the 'significant fringe competition' exists at all if the dominant firm's cost advantage is substantial. Secondly, if nevertheless fringe firms can find a place in the market, driving them out by exclusionary or predatory pricing is likely to have only a short-run effect. As soon as the dominant firm raises its prices in order to recoup previous profits foregone by its low pricing strategy entry will recur, and again capture a significant market share. Thirdly, while there is evidence that dominant firms have used such exclusionary tactics from time to time, this has most frequently been where the dominant firm was practically a monopolist and therefore was assured of a quick victory with little loss to itself (see Utton, 1979, chapter 5). Just as, therefore, a dominant firm may find it advantageous to acquire smaller rivals to reverse the erosion of its market share, it may also prevent successful entry by temporarily cutting prices below the entrant's (or in the limit its own) costs, and hence for a period make very low returns despite its large market share.

The dominant firm will be aware that either of these policies are likely to make it the target for antitrust action[6] and, as a number of writers have suggested, prefer the less overtly aggressive option of limit pricing which may result in only small profit sacrifices (Scherer, 1980, pp. 238–9). If the threat of competition (and antitrust policy) leads firms with large market shares to restrain their prices persistently below the short-run profit maximising level this raises an important policy question. Although the structure of the industry is nearer 'monopoly' than 'competition', given the state of technology and possibly economies of scale in distribution and marketing, is the industry nevertheless performing as well as any of the feasible alternatives? Fisher (1979), for example, has recently argued that if dominant firms are in effect forced to choose limit pricing as their optimal strategy then competition is working even though it might remain potential rather than actual. 'Where competitors are forced out or entry forestalled only by prices being kept low, competition is doing its job' (p. 30). If this is then overlaid with the kind of dynamic forces stressed by the Austrian writers and accepted to a greater or lesser extent by others,[7] then industrial performance may be as good as is compatible with economies of scale in production and the requirements of innovation.[8]

A central conclusion from the discussion of the pricing policies of dominant firms (or groups) and the effect of entry barriers is that at any one time, for a cross-section of markets, the shares of the leading firms will reflect a number of different influences. Some may be newly established and protected by legal constraints (such as a patent), others may still be substantial but in the process of erosion from new entry or expansion by fringe competitors (the rate of which will vary from market to market) while another group may be maintained by an uneasy policy of limit pricing.

In view of these different circumstances, although we might expect very large market shares to be associated with above competitive rates of return, the relationship may not be very clear-cut, especially if some firms have had to adopt defensive strategies to maintain their position. Pashigian (1968), similarly, concludes his analysis of limit pricing and the market share of the leading firm by explaining that 'there is nothing in the theory which suggests a monotonically increasing relationship between market share and rate of return' (p. 176). Any relationship might be further clouded in practice by the prevalence of X-inefficiency amongst those leading firms which feel themselves sufficiently protected from competition to allow part of what would otherwise be an abnormal return to be consumed by internal slack.

Others, however, have argued differently and reached quite different conclusions. Shepherd (1972, 1975), in his analysis of market power, has placed market share at the centre of the stage. He suggests that market share of the leading firm is likely to be the most important aspect of market structure and be directly related to profitability. It will reflect three underlying influences: market power, especially the increased ability of dominant firms to discriminate on prices; technical economies of scale in production; and pecuniary economies particularly in dealings with input suppliers. The relationship between profitability and 'market power' is likely to be monotonically increasing although probably at a declining rate as dominant firms find it more and more difficult or ill-advised to increase their share beyond a certain point. Pecuniary economies are likely to grow more significant the greater the market share while technical economies, apart from a few industries, may tend to peter out beyond a certain point and even lead to X-inefficiency, so that the profitability–market share relationship for this element alone may be more ambiguous. But, Shepherd concludes, 'On balance, the share–profit relationship is expected to be upward-sloping and possibly convex. By contrast, Cournot-type analysis (especially by Worcester) suggests a low or zero slope for the relationship' (p. 43). Clearly such a conflict of hypotheses can only be resolved empirically. For much of the 1950s and 1960s, particularly under the stimulus given by Bain's work, most empirical research looked at a number of *industry* characteristics and their relationship with performance rather than observing *firm* characteristics and in particular the influence of market share. More recently a number of studies, mainly in the United States, have shifted the emphasis back to the firm. We review the main results of this work in the next section.

EMPIRICAL STUDIES OF MARKET SHARES

Most of the empirical studies have been concerned with the short-to-medium term, ranging from periods of three to ten years. Although in some cases the analysis has been explicitly short-term, in most the main reason for confining the study to a relatively short period has been problems with data. Market share data, defined in a way consistent with the theoretical analysis and also systematically for a large enough sample of markets and for a number of different years, are generally not available. In a number of cases the researcher has had to rely on special tabulations or on approximations.

Some of the earlier studies which focused on market shares were mainly concerned to re-establish their importance as an aspect of market structure and their probable superiority to market concentration. While concentration, usually measured by the ratio of sales of the largest four or five firms to total sales, might give a first indication of where oligopolistic collusion was most likely to be found, it gave no idea of the market share differences of the leading firms. In addition concentration statistics for different years do not show how the position of the market leaders might be changing over time.

The writer who perhaps more than any other has recently emphasised the importance of market shares is Shepherd (1972, 1975, 1979). He has attempted to examine both the long-run stability of market shares in oligopoly, as well as the relationship between profitability and market share. On the basis of estimates of the changing market position for twenty American firms over the period 1910 to 1935 and for eighteen firms (some the same) between 1948 and 1973 he draws the following conclusions; first, the decline of market share was on average generally much greater where the firm had been affected in some way by public policy (for example antitrust action or lapse of a patent); secondly, the rate of market share erosion was approximately five times as great in the earlier period as in the later period for those firms not affected by policy;[9] and thirdly, leading market positions in 1976 were 'of several decades standing or more', but that 'the erosion process does appear to work in most of the rest of industry and trade except where specific devices limit competition' (patents, franchises, and so on) (1979, p. 208). To this extent, therefore, there is support for the Worcester view, discussed above, that 'dominant' firms in particular markets do decline over time although this may be at varying rates in different time periods and directly affected by policy measures.

The main thrust of Shepherd's analysis, however, has been into the relationship between profitability and market share. Some of the hypotheses discussed in the previous section incorporated directly or indirectly the notion that profitability will be positively related to market share. He estimated the relationship between profitability (average 1960–9 return on equity) and average market share together with other variables reflecting market structure.[10] What emerged most clearly from his work and similar papers by Dalton and Levin (1977), Gale (1972), and Kwoka (1979), is the strong direct relationship between profitability and market share. He emphasised that the model of market structure and performance that he was testing concerned the short-to-medium term and not what he called 'life-cycle and profit-growth choices' for which he cited the evidence on the maintenance or erosion of market shares over the long period (Shepherd, 1975, chapter 4).

If, however, the statistical results are, for the most part, short-term,[11] the policy implications which Shepherd considered at length do not seem to follow. He concluded, for example, that on average each additional 10 percentage points to market share will increase the rate of return by 2.5 per cent. But if these higher returns are short-lived because of the normal process of competition, then there is little need for a policy response and certainly none for the direct attack on market share of dominant firms which he later advocated.

A further point concerns the way in which the key variable was measured in the above studies. In all cases firm 'market share' consisted of a weighted average of estimated market shares across the markets in which the firm operated.[12] In the context of measuring the possible effects of market power it is not clear what such a variable means, especially since most samples were drawn from the largest American companies, many of which are now highly diversified (even if the pure conglomerates are omitted). The impact of any market power effect is thus almost bound to be weakened by the use of such weighted averages.

Furthermore, the shift away from *industry* cross-sections to those of *firms* has also unfortunately meant in some cases (for example, Dalton and Levin, 1977 and Gale, 1972) a reintroduction into the statistical analysis of weighted average concentration ratios as a further explanatory variable. In view of the criticisms that have been made of such a measure when trying to measure structure–performance relationships using multiple regression analysis, its renewed use is, to say the least, surprising (Scherer, 1980, p. 270). It would be unfortunate if the whole debate were to be repeated over the correct measure of market share.

As Scherer concludes: 'Far more suitable for pinpointing the relative roles of industry structure and firm market shares are data disaggregated to the level of individual sellers' lines of business' (p. 283). Ideally, of course, because of the diversification of many large enterprises and the complexity of their internal sales, to test the relationship between market share and profitability *both* variables should relate quite strictly to a properly identified 'market' rather than to an amalgamation of different markets. As we shall see below the great advantage of the Monopolies Commission data is that they come very close to meeting this requirement both for market share and profitability.

OUTLINE OF THE STUDY

A major source of information used throughout the study is thus the reports of the Monopolies and Mergers Commission. Data from the reports are used extensively in chapter 2 to test a number of hypotheses concerning the relationship between market shares and profitability. The special attraction of the data is that they relate very closely to markets rather than to more broadly defined industries. The problems that are usually encountered, therefore, of trying to measure the profitability of large, possibly diversified, companies for just one of its product ranges can be largely overcome. It is thus possible to compare the relative profitability of market leaders and market followers, and to measure the overall relationship between market shares and profitability.

In chapter 3 we turn from examining the essentially short-run relationship between profitability and market shares, to a consideration of the long-run pattern of change, especially amongst dominant firms. The weight of the theoretical analysis suggests that in the long run competitive forces of one kind or another will tend to erode market shares although, as we show, Williamson has recently argued that in a sizeable minority of cases, dominance may be permanent unless strong antitrust action is taken to counter it. We examine this issue first, with a small sample originally used by Stigler and now updated to cover the greater part of this century, and then with a larger sample covering approximately the period from the Second World War to the late 1970s. Although the evidence on the whole supports the erosion hypothesis, it is also clear that dominant firms usually retain their leadership position and a sizeable market share for long periods, despite suffering a relative decline. The chapter also examines the impact of imports and mergers on positions of dominance, the former as potentially an important source of increased competition and the latter as a means of reversing a decline in market share. The sample underlines the need for information on whether imports are truly competitive with domestic output. It also shows that the *net* effect of mergers in markets dominated by one firm may be neutral, although clearly in individual cases their impact has been important.

The suggestion in chapter 2 that market leaders and market followers in different kinds of oligopoly may have similar relative profit levels, even though profits as between oligopolies are different, prompted the analysis of chapter 4. Using concentration data for the period 1958–77, we examine the hypothesis that firms in oligopoly collude (tacitly) to raise prices above competitive levels. If this is the case it would account for the similar profit levels of firms with different market shares and it would also lead to a decline over time in the combined market share of leaders in heavily concentrated markets greater than that expected from the normal process of regression.

The final chapter summarises the main results and makes some tentative policy proposals, all of which could be carried out within the existing framework. In particular we emphasise the need to extend the coverage of market share indices for a wide range of products and on a regular basis so as to supplement the concentration data that is already available. Although it is not possible for the Business Statistics Office to publish information concerning individual firms, it should be feasible for them, possibly in collaboration with the Office of Fair Trading, to devise indices of market share instability for groups of the largest firms.

2

PROFITABILITY AND MARKET SHARES

INTRODUCTION

Many studies that have attempted to measure the relationship between market structure and performance have shown a weak positive correlation between profitability and the level of concentration, holding other factors constant. The observations have usually been at the industry level (rather than the firm level) and have been interpreted as giving modest support to the hypothesis that firms in more heavily concentrated industries can collude effectively to maintain joint profits above competitive levels. The supposition is that the larger the joint market share of the leading group of firms in a market, the easier it will be for them to maintain the discipline necessary for positive margins: the smaller the number of firms involved the easier the detection of 'cheating' on prices and hence the lower the incentive for members of the group to attempt to engage in such tactics (see chapter 4 for a more detailed examination of this hypothesis). Implicit, therefore, in such *industry* studies has been the assumption that *firm* market share will be correlated with profitability. In some recent studies, to which we referred above, explicit account was taken of this relationship and the focus of attention shifted from the industry to the firm.

The relationship between profitability and market share has been extensively studied by Shepherd (1972 and 1975). His argument, which we set out in more detail in the next section, centres both on the increased opportunities for collusion which large market shares may bring and also on the lower unit costs achieved by large-scale production and marketing. Opponents of the first part of this hypothesis have criticised the notion that large market shares are any guarantee of high profits. They deny that large market shares make successful collusion feasible while accepting that they do make for efficiency. Indeed they argue that any correlation between profitability and market share rests precisely on the efficiency and progressivenesss of the firms concerned (see, for example, Brozen, 1982, and Demsetz, 1973).

Although they disagree on the reasons underlying the relationship, they seem to agree that it is well established empirically, at least for the United States. Yet as we point out in the third section of this chapter, the data on which this conclusion rests are far from ideal. Information relating to properly identified markets is notoriously difficult to collect and most American studies have therefore had to rely, especially for profitability, on data at a much higher level of aggregation than the hypothesis implies. (Other studies have used highly disaggregated data collected directly from firms but these have a number of other problems to which we refer below.) Many of these problems can be overcome by using data assembled in Monopolies and Mergers Commission reports and these are also discussed in the third section of this chapter. This is followed by a more detailed exploration of the relationship between market shares and profitability in the United Kingdom.

THE RELATIONSHIP BETWEEN PROFITABILITY AND MARKET SHARES

For firms operating in 'competitive' markets where entry is easy and market shares very small, the intensity of the rivalry will ensure that average profit rates are kept to the minimum necessary to retain productive capacity. At the other extreme a single seller will be able, by simple or discriminatory pricing, to earn abnormal returns if entry is barred and if the firm maintains its internal efficiency. Between these two polar cases there is likely to be an exceedingly complex relationship between profitability and market share.

For simplicity Shepherd starts his discussion of the relationship between market share and profitability in terms of a linear function with the vertical intercept representing the 'competitive' rate of return. Underlying the simple relation are three factors: technical economies of scale, pecuniary economies and market power. For manufacturing industries he argues that the relationship between technical economies and profits is likely to be positive up to the point where the economies are exhausted (and unit production costs become horizontal). Thereafter the influence on profits may be either zero or possibly negative if coordination or other administrative problems lead to X-inefficiency (see Shepherd, 1979, especially pp. 177–9). He envisages the influence of pecuniary economies (essentially the financial advantages of bargaining and buying on a large scale) on profitability as generally positive throughout the relevant market share range, although beyond a certain point additional positive effects, in the form of reduced costs, may be negligible.

The market power effect makes itself felt through the greater capacity firms will have to increase their profits through various forms of price discrimination, according to Shepherd. But, in its turn, this ability will depend on the confidence of firms in the oligopolistic group that there is sufficient mutual understanding between them for individual price policies not to be misunderstood. The degree of cohesiveness will increase with the size of the market shares of the leading firms. The fewer the firms the greater the likely control of total output and therefore the greater the capacity to earn abnormal returns. Beyond a certain size of market share, however, the relationship may be weakened. First, it may become increasingly costly and even unwise to push an individual market share towards the monopolistic limit. Secondly, sales pushed into the outer 'limits' of a market are more and more likely to encounter active competition from firms previously regarded merely as potential rivals.

The net effect of these influences, therefore, is likely to produce a positive though not necessarily linear relationship between profitability and market share. But other structural features of the market are likely to complicate the relationship. First, for given current market shares, profitability will be lower the smaller the barriers to entry. Thus, in a market with low entry barriers existing market shares, even sizeable ones, will only be retained if entry is forestalled by charging low prices which yield competitive returns. Markets with similarly distributed leading shares but with different entry conditions are thus likely to produce different rates of profit. Secondly, it is sometimes argued that regardless of existing shares in a particular market the overall (or conglomerate) size of the parent company will give an added advantage. The profitability of firms with particular market shares in a given market will therefore be higher (*ceteris paribus*) if they are members of a much larger grouping than if they are largely dependent on the one market for their survival.

Another group of writers arrives at essentially the same conclusion of a positive association between market share and profitability but using a different route and with different implications. The focus of their attention is more particularly the market leaders rather than all firms in the industry. Thus Brozen (1982, p. 211) specifically argues that 'a large market share does not confer market power' but the leaders only maintain their position as long as they are technically efficient and progressive. If they are, then they will also be profitable and any observed correlation between market share and profits is simply a reflection of efficiency and dynamism. On the other hand, leading firms that attempt to exploit what they believe to be an impregnable position by charging high prices so as to maintain their profits will suffer a loss of market share to competitors. Both Brozen and Demsetz (1973a) conclude that the empirical evidence tends to suggest that leading firms generally choose the former course of action to maintain their profits rather than the latter. In chapter 3 we attempt to analyse the long-term market share changes in leading firms for a sample of markets. For the moment, however, we may note that, whereas the Shepherd analysis of market shares and profitability rests at least partially on abuses of market power with the implication that a positive policy response may be required,[1] the Brozen analysis leads to the conclusion that any attack on the market shares of leading firms will be at the expense of efficiency and progressiveness.

PROFITABILITY AND MARKET SHARE: DATA

In his ambitious study of the relationship Shepherd used data for 245 of the largest American manufacturing enterprises. The results are discussed in greatest detail and extended in his book called *The Treatment of Market Power* (1975). One of the main results was of a strong positive relation between average firm profitability and weighted average market share, holding other structural characteristics constant. (These included the combined share of the leading group, without the firm observed, overall firm size, advertising intensity and firm growth rate.) The regression coefficient for market share was 'about 0.25 which means that there is on average a 2.5 per cent higher rate of return on equity for each added ten points of market share' (Shepherd, 1979, p. 195). The result has been used extensively by Shepherd to estimate the degree of market power of dominant firms; that is, the profit rate that the firms would have realised if their market share and entry barriers exerted their normal influence. Subsequent work by Gale and Branch (1982) and Kwoka (1978) has also emphasised the importance of market shares, although in the latter case only the two leading shares in a market seemed directly related to profitability while the third share had the wrong sign.

Although these studies used different sources of basic data, one characteristic they all have in common is that profitability figures related to the whole of the firms' activities not just to those of particular markets. Consequently the market share measures had to be a weighted average of the firms' complete range of market shares which typically had to be estimated from incomplete data. Since the firms involved were usually amongst the largest in the American manufacturing sector, many of them were highly diversified. The profit and market share data related to a whole profile of possibly disparate activities and this would tend to obscure the fundamental relationship under investigation which refers specifically to *market* share and *market* profitability. Ideally our observation should clearly relate to individual markets, rather than to averages across a number of markets. A firm large in absolute terms operating in many markets with differing shares will earn different rates of return according to its market share, if the fundamental relationship holds.

The central advantage, therefore, of using data from the reports of the Monopolies and Mergers Commission (MMC) is that these refer to markets, narrowly defined.[2] The market share data probably came as close as is feasible in practice to the theoretical concept of a market. Similarly, in many reports, rates of return on capital are published which relate as strictly as possible to that part of the enterprise's activities under review. Even though the firm with the leading share may be part of a much larger organisation the profit figures will relate only to the market concerned. For example, Unilever, ranked ninth overall amongst United Kingdom quoted enterprises in the middle 1970s, had leading shares in three of the markets in the sample, ice cream, detergents and frozen foods, but market share and rate of return on capital figures are given individually for each case.

In both respects, therefore, profits and market share, the MMC data are superior to those which have to be taken from the whole enterprise. There are also, however, a number of drawbacks. First, the markets investigated by the MMC are a non-random sample where there is some ground for expecting possible abuses of market power, although the MMC itself must treat each reference to it in a neutral fashion. There is no presumption on its part that the firm or firms concerned are acting against the public interest. Nevertheless it remains true that, say, the degree of concentration in the markets referred to the MMC is considerably higher than for industry generally.[3] Secondly, and more seriously, only relatively few MMC reports are published each year. Consequently, although a substantial number of cases is available, the data relate to different years because of the timing of publication. In most of the analysis that follows, therefore, profitability is taken *relative* to that for manufacturing industry as a whole (the details are set out more fully below). A third limitation follows directly from the second point. Many other factors, in addition to market share, may affect profitability. Much empirical research has been undertaken, for example, to explore the relationship between profitability and market concentration, product differentiation, productivity and trade levels (see in particular Comanor and Wilson, 1974, and Hart and Clarke, 1980). For the most part this work has been carried out at a level of aggregation (the three digit industry) which allows the simultaneous observation of a multivariate relationship but which, because of the breadth of most of the industries included, strays somewhat from the individual *market*, the main focus of this study. On the other hand, while the data on market shares and profitability from the Monopolies and Mergers Commission come close to what is ideally required, data on other variables which may affect the relationship are generally not available on a comparable basis. For this reason most of the subsequent analysis is bivariate rather than multivariate. A fourth objection that may be raised against using the data in MMC reports to examine the question in hand is that since they come from an 'antitrust' source they are likely to be biased downwards. Firms in a prominent position in a particular market anticipating the close attention of the Office of Fair Trading can, on this view, take steps to disguise the true position by recording lower profits than actually earned in the hope that this will forestall an expensive inquiry. Although this possibility should be recognised, its practical impact is likely to be slight. The enterprises referred to the MMC do not learn much in advance either that they are being considered or which particular market of theirs may be involved. Also, once the inquiry has commenced, the financial analysis is carried out by the MMC's own trained accountants. It is reasonably well established that large, diversified firms have detailed and decentralised monitoring systems for their own internal purposes and much of the data published in the final MMC reports is probably derived from these records. The quality of the information is therefore likely to be as good as can be obtained both for market share and profitability.[4]

In recent years the MMC has increasingly called for asset valuations to be calculated on a current cost basis so as to take reasonable account of inflation. For a sample confined to, say, the last five years, rates of return on capital estimated in this way would be available. Since, however, we wished to use reports going back over a much longer period in order to widen the sample we have had to use profitability figures related to assets based on historic cost. As long as all comparisons are made on the same basis no major bias should be introduced from this source, but clearly rates of return will appear generally higher than they would have been using a current cost base.

PROFITABILITY AND MARKET SHARES IN THREE TYPES OF OLIGOPOLY

Inclusion in the sample clearly required that sufficient information on market shares and profitability was published in the relevant report. Also we used the cut-off points of 1960–1 and 1980–1, so reports published in the early 1960s but referring to the late 1950s were not included. On this basis we were able to assemble data on 52 different products which for present purposes are treated as separate 'markets' although we are aware that in some instances the product is too narrowly defined and in others too widely defined to match the theoretical ideal (see also Scherer, 1980, pp. 59–64). The three categories into which they were initially grouped were as follows: dominant firm, concentrated oligopoly, and loose oligopoly. In the first category the leading firm had a market share of 50 per cent or more and the second ranked firm had to have a share of less than half that of the market leader. This group, therefore, should conform fairly closely to the dominant firm model of economic theory where the market leader has considerable discretion in its pricing policies, although it may have to take due account of the likely outputs offered by fringe suppliers at various prices.[5] The factors mentioned by Shepherd, especially the influence of market power, should be at their strongest for members of this group. In the second category we have tried to include markets shared between two large firms so that opportunities for cooperation rather than conflict are most likely to produce high rates of return. The two leading firms had to share 50 per cent or more of the market to qualify for this group. It also included cases where the market leader had more than half the market but where the second ranked firm had a share more than half as great as the first. The market was thus much more akin to duopoly than the dominant firm case. Finally in the third group we included the remaining cases where the two leading firms shared less than half the market and where frequently there was little difference between the market shares of the leading four or five firms.

It is clear from the description of the three groups that our sample is taken from the more concentrated half of markets in manufacturing industry. There is no representation of markets where the largest four or five firms account for as little as one quarter or a third of the total. The bias stems from the source of most of the data. Nevertheless there is still sufficient differentiation in basic market structure for the relationship between profitability and market share to show up in the sample if it actually holds in practice. As Stigler (1966, p. 217) remarks, 'Almost every economist believes that an industry with two (and certainly with five) firms behaves differently from a monopoly'.

To determine whether the firms in the three groups distinguished behave differently enough to produce distinct rates of profit, we have had to relate the rates of return on capital (usually taken over five years)[6] to a suitable base since, as we mentioned above, the profit figures refer to different periods depending on when the MMC reports were published. For this purpose we have used the series published in various issues of the Business Monitor on Company Finance to estimate the average rate of return on capital for quoted companies in manufacturing industry for the period 1960 to 1980. (More details of this series are given in appendix 2 to this chapter). The average rates of return earned by the leading firms in the three groups were then expressed as a proportion of the average for quoted companies in manufacturing industry for the relevant period. We are thus implicitly assuming that whatever their market share, leading firms can respond equally to cyclical influences on general profitability. (The reliability of this procedure is discussed more fully in the following section.)

The result of these calculations for the three groups is set out in table 2.1. Note at this stage we are comparing the relative profitability of only the *leading* firm in each market. We consider below the related question of whether there is any difference between profit rates for market leaders and market followers within each group.

The share of the market leaders in the first group was on average more

Table 2.1 *Relative profitability of leading firms in three types of oligopoly*

Group	Number of markets	Average market share of leader (%)[a]	Average profit relative[b, c]
Dominant firm	19[d]	72.9	2.03 (0.95)
Concentrated oligopoly	21	39.6	1.53 (0.68)
Loose oligopoly	9	26.1	1.16 (0.76)
Total	49	50.1	1.66 (0.86)

Source: Appendix 2.1.

[a] Usually averaged over five years. See appendix 2.1 for more details.

[b] Average rate of return on capital relative to the average for quoted manufacturing companies.

[c] Standard deviations in brackets.

[d] Three extreme observations omitted from the table. The conclusion is confirmed if they are included. See Note 7 to chapter 2.

than three-quarters as big again as those of the leaders in the second group, while the average market share of leaders in the third group was about two-thirds of those in the second group. The relative profitability figures in the third column of the table suggest that market leaders in the dominant firm group were able to earn, on average, profits about twice the level for quoted companies in manufacturing industry, while firms in the concentrated oligopoly group managed profits about one and a half times the industry average. Where oligopolistic interdependence may have been much less, in the third group, profits were only 16 per cent above the manufacturing industry average. Using a standard analysis of variance test for differences between the mean profit relatives suggests that the differences were significant at the 5 per cent level.[7]

There is thus some preliminary support for the view that profitability and market share are directly related, at least as far as the market leaders are concerned, and if the more general characteristics of the oligopolistic market structure are taken into account. It may indicate that a very large market share not only confers on the leader substantial economies of scale but also allows discretion over price. Where the market is shared more or less equally between two or three firms, as in the second group, incomplete coordination of policies and intermittent intense rivalry may restrain profit levels, although these are still on average 50 per cent or so above the 'normal' level. In the 'loose oligopoly' category for which we only have nine cases, competition may be sufficiently acute to keep average profits closer to the normal level, although it should be remembered that members of this group are still firmly in the *oligopoly* class (it includes, for example, bread, ready mixed concrete, frozen foods and beer; a complete list is given in appendix 2.1 to this chapter).

A related question and one which has recently been at the centre of a considerable amount of controversy, is whether the relatively high profits earned by leaders in concentrated markets also apply to firms with smaller market shares. In particular Demsetz (1973a) has argued that if *collusion* in oligopoly is really the explanation for observed correlations between profitability and concentration, then firms with small market shares should also earn high profits as their reward for tacit participation in cooperative policies that avoid competition. On the other hand, if the higher profits for the market leaders are due to their efficiency in production and ability in meeting consumer demands, then smaller firms in the markets concerned should earn *lower* profits, because they are likely to be less efficient.[8] Demsetz then presents some evidence from United States manufacturing industry which supports his contention. A subsequent study by Round (1975), using Australian data, appeared to confirm these results. Demsetz argued that his results also helped to explain the frequently observed positive association between profits or price cost margins and concentration in multivariate cross-section studies. In concentrated industries most of the profits earned will be by the larger firms. Consequently it is these profits that contribute to the positive association but if they are really attributable to efficiency rather than collusion, the policy implications are quite different from those usually drawn. In particular any attempt at deconcentration (or possibly merger prevention) may sacrifice efficiency.

His conclusions have not, however, gone unchallenged. Some writers have questioned the appropriateness of the statistical techniques employed (see Bond and Greenberg, 1976, and Rosenbluth, 1976), while Porter (1979) has offered an alternative interpretation in terms of 'strategic groups' within industries which may explain the observed differences between profit rates for different groups of firms of the same industry. Unfortunately the notion of a 'strategic group' within an industry seems very much to depend on how the industry is defined. The three digit industry level used by Porter in his analysis may be much too broad for our purposes with its focus on distinct, narrowly defined *markets*. One point that Porter makes, however, is relevant. He observes that, 'my results show that in many industries the leading firms are not the most profitable at all' (p. 227) and that this is inconsistent with Demsetz's hypothesis. The same point can be made about the United Kingdom data. In 21 of the markets in the sample, market share and profit data are given not only

Table 2.2 *Highest profit relatives in 21 markets*

Market	Firm	Market share (%)	Profit relative
Markets where the market leader had the highest profits			
Ice cream	Unilever	47.5	1.93
Cat and dog food	Pedigree Petfoods	50.3	3.11
Domestic gas appliances	Thorn	34.7	1.51
Bread	Rank, Hovis, McDougall	24.2	0.32
Frozen food	Unilever	33.5	1.22
Beer	Bass	20.0	1.01
Savoury snack foods	United Biscuits	30.0	1.58
Markets where a market 'follower' had the highest profits			
Flour	ABF	19.4 (3)[a]	2.95
Detergents	Procter and Gamble	42.2 (2)	4.21
Meters	GEC	20.6 (4)	2.33
Winding wires	AEI	32.0 (2)	0.83
Electric lamps	GEC	20.5 (3)	1.65
Ceramic sanitary ware	Ideal Standard	18.5 (3)	1.74
Concrete roofing tiles	Sandtoft Tileries	8.1 (3)	3.72
Glass bottles	Redfearn National Glass	16.5 (3)	1.32
Rolls for rolling mills	Davy International	33.6 (3)	1.39
Cement	Rugby Portland	15.0 (3)	1.73
Industrial gases	Air Products	20.0 (2)	1.60
General wiring cable	AEI	6.6 (4)	1.65
Ready mixed concrete	Pioneer Concrete	9.7 (3)	2.92
Petrol distribution	Esso	19.0 (2)	0.73

Source: Appendix 2.1.

[a] The figures in brackets give the market share rank of the company cited, according to the MMC reports.

for the leaders but also for at least one other firm with a smaller share. But, since only two cases (cement and industrial gases) come from the dominant firm group, any conclusions must be tentative since it is possible that had data on the profitability of smaller companies in more of these markets been available they might have been below the level of the market leader.[9] Of the other cases twelve came from the concentrated oligopoly group and seven from the loose oligopoly group. In no less than fourteen cases the profit relative of the market leader was below that of the smaller firm. The details of these cases are set out in table 2.2. In eight cases in the lower part of the table the firm with the highest profitability was ranked third or fourth according to market share.[10] These cases, therefore, tend to go against the Demsetz view that high profits (in concentrated markets) are a reflection of efficiency due in part to scale economies, although in some cases like detergents, winding wires and rolls for rolling mills the market share of the second ranked firm was so large (one third or more) that it is consistent with his view.

The hypothesis can be considered further by comparing the profit relatives of the market leaders with *all* other firms in each oligopolistic group for which information is available. Although it can only be a partial test because of the composition of the sample,[11] we should still expect a noticeable difference between the relative profitability of the market leaders and that of other firms, some of which will have considerably smaller market shares, if Demsetz is correct. On the other hand, if some degree of collusion exists between firms in oligopoly, all firms should benefit and no differences in relative profitability should be observed between the market leaders and others.

The results of this comparison are set out in table 2.3. We have to confine the comparison to the second and third oligopoly groups, since profit and market share data for firms other than the market leader are, as mentioned above, only available for *two* markets in the first group. Although the average market shares of non-market leaders in both groups were much smaller than those of the market leaders, there was very little difference between their relative profitabilities. For the thirteen market leaders in the concentrated oligopoly group the average profit relative was 1.55 compared with 1.36 for the 26 non-market leaders, while in the loose oligopoly group, the market leaders average profit relative was 1.07 compared with 0.94 for other firms in the group. The difference in both cases was about 14 per cent and is in the direction that Demsetz predicts: market leaders earn more, on average, than smaller firms operating in the same market. (Neither of the differences is, however, statistically significant.) With fuller information both from dominant firms' markets and those of much lower concentration the differences might have been more marked.

On the other hand, supporters of the conventional view that all firms in oligopoly enjoy higher prices because of collusion could argue that the differences observed in table 2.3 are so slight as to support their contention. If leading firms owe their higher profits mainly to efficiency compared with smaller firms in their markets then there should be no difference between the relative profitability of the non-market leaders in both groups, yet non-leaders in the concentrated oligopoly group earned relative profits 45 per cent higher than non-leaders in the loose oligopoly group (1.36 against 0.94). Furthermore, since the average market share of non-leaders in the concentrated oligopoly group is not much less than that of the leaders in the loose oligopoly group they might be expected to earn similar profits.

Table 2.3 *Relative profitability of leading firms and other firms in two types of oligopoly*

Group	Number of firms	Average market share (%)	Average profit relative
Concentrated oligopoly			
Market leader	13	38.1	1.55 (0.79)[a]
Others	26	21.1	1.36 (1.00)
Loose oligopoly			
Market leader	6	27.3	1.07 (0.85)
Others	14[b]	11.7	0.94 (0.96)

Source: Appendix 2.1.

[a] Standard deviations in brackets.

[b] Three firms with market shares of under 4 per cent in the ready mixed concrete market were not included in this calculation since four other firms were already included. The conclusion in the text is reinforced if they are included.

In fact, however, as table 2.3 shows, relative profits for the former group are 27 per cent higher (that is, 1.36 compared with 1.07) than the latter group (although the difference is not significant).

So far, therefore, the analysis of the market share and profitability data suggests that oligopoly type does have a positive effect on relative profits, at least for the market leaders. Very often, however, firms ranked second or third by market share earn higher returns than the market leader. This point, together with some evidence (in table 2.3) that there are comparatively slight profitability differences between market leaders and others within oligopolistic groups, tends to work against the Demsetz view.

REGRESSION ANALYSIS OF PROFITABILITY AND MARKET SHARE

In the light of the results of the previous section it seems likely that the relationship between profitability and market share is rather complex. Yet there is a growing body of evidence from the United States that supports the view of a clear positive association, *ceteris paribus* (see in particular Gale and Branch, 1982, Shepherd, 1975, and, with modifications, Kwoka, 1978). Lacking information on profitability by individual market these studies have had to use profitability for the whole enterprise with a weighted average of market shares.

Table 2.4 *Simple regression of relative profitability on market share*

	Equation number	Number of observations	Constant	Coefficient[a]	r^2
Control sample	(1)	42	0.337 (0.270)	0.030[b] (0.008)	0.282
Full sample	(2)	97	0.733 (0.189)	0.023[b] (0.004)	0.223
Dominant firm group	(3)	22	−0.721 (1.714)	0.042 (0.023)	0.147
Concentrated oligopoly					
Market leaders only	(4)	21	1.312 (0.805)	0.006 (0.020)	0.004
All firms	(5)	45	0.708 (0.304)	0.023[c] (0.009)	0.119
Loose oligopoly					
All firms	(6)	27	0.908 (0.317)	0.006 (0.018)	0.005

[a] Standard errors in brackets.
[b] Significant at the 1 per cent level.
[c] Significant at the 5 per cent level.

In order to test the relationship for British industry we have used the data assembled from the various MMC and other official reports discussed in the previous section and set out in the appendix to this chapter. We have already discussed the reason for using a profit *relative* as the dependent variable (p. 13 above) rather than, say, the average rate of return on capital. But in order to test the reliability of this measure we were able to form a sub-sample of 42 firms for which market share and profitability data were all available for the same period, 1972–4. These years were chosen simply because they maximised the number of observations available for a common time interval. The sub-sample was then used as a control group in the following way. If the statistical results were the same for the sub-sample as for the full sample (which draws on data for different years) then we would regard this as supporting the use of profit relatives as the dependent variable. If the results were quite different this would suggest that the profit relative was unreliable.[12]

The simple regressions of relative profitability on market share for the full sample and control group are given in the first part of table 2.4. In both cases the regression coefficient is highly significant, suggesting that there is a clear, positive association between relative profitability and market share. The fact that the results for the full sample are similar to those for the control group suggests that no undue distortion arises from the use of the *relative* profit variable constructed from rates of return covering different periods. About one quarter of inter-firm relative profitability variation may be explained by difference in market share.

In the previous section stratifying the sample suggested that there was a direct association between relative profitability, market share and type of oligopoly, with market leaders in the dominant firm group earning significantly higher profits than those in more loose-knit oligopolies. We can now examine whether the relationship between relative profitability and market share holds *within* each group. Do firms with the largest market shares in the dominant firm group for example earn higher relative profits than others, with smaller market shares, in the same group? The results are given in the second and third parts of table 2.4. Equations (3) and (4) refer to the market leaders only in the two oligopoly groups specified. The third group was not included as there were only nine observations. Equations (5) and (6) include *all* firms in the two groups shown.

As far as the dominant firm group is concerned there is some indication that a bigger market share might tend to increase relative profits. The size of the regression coefficient is fairly similar to those in equations (1) and (2) but the small sample size gives a larger standard error. Even so the coefficient only just fails to be significant at the 5 per cent level (the *t* ratio was 1.83).

The implications of this result (if it is accepted) are interesting. It suggests that firms with a considerable market share (remember that market leaders in this group have 50 per cent or more of a narrowly defined market) are likely to continue to have a strong profit incentive to *increase* their share even more, either by internal growth or acquisition. It implies that they are unlikely to yield up market share without a considerable struggle. Theories that predict the decline of dominant firms' share of the market (for example, Worcester, 1957) usually incorporate a process of gradual erosion due to new entry, the rate of which may be controlled by the dominant firm itself. Dewey (1959) has made the additional point that beyond a certain (high) market share, further increments are likely to be very costly both in terms of the competitive intensity generated and the policy response that aggressive action by a dominant firm may provoke. Both observations were made against the background of American antitrust policy. In the United Kingdom, where antitrust remedies are mild or non-existent by comparison, the arguments may have much less force. A threatened market share may be maintained by a strategic acquisition which, although apparently bringing only a minor addition to the acquirer's total market share at the time, may nevertheless prevent subsequent erosion. We examine this question for a sample of markets in chapter 3.

Turning to equation (4) which refers to market leaders in the concentrated oligopoly group, the relationship between relative profits and market share disappears altogether. Thus, although market leaders in this group earn higher profits, on average, than leaders in less concentrated markets (table 2.1), there appears to be no systematic relationship between profitability and market share for market leaders *within* the concentrated oligopoly group. The explanation for this can be seen if we compare the result in equation (5) with that of equation (4). If non-market leaders in the concentrated oligopoly are included (equation 5) in the analysis, then the regression coefficient is again significant (at the 5 per cent level). Within this type of oligopoly where two to four firms may have roughly equal shares and dominate the market, a major influence on relative profits will be the intensity of competition amongst the leading firms. In one market a share of, say, 40 per cent may allow high profits to be earned because of the comparative lack of effective competition while a similar market share may lead to quite different profits where competition is intense. Ready Mixed Concrete, for example, with a share of 34 per cent of the market, earned profits two and a half times the manufacturing industry average whereas BLI with a very similar share of the electric lamp market earned no surplus profits at all. Whereas the second largest firm in the former market had a share of only 13 per cent, in the electric lamp market the equivalent share was 24 per cent. For market leaders in this group there is thus no well defined relationship between profitability and market share.

The inclusion of other firms in addition to the market leaders re-establishes, however, the underlying relationship shown in equations (1) and (2). We have already observed (table 2.2) that in fourteen markets in the sample the non-leader, in terms of market share, had the highest relative profits. Eight of these cases occurred in the concentrated oligopoly group but quite often the share of the second or third ranked firm, which also earned the highest profits in the market concerned, was only marginally below that of the market leader. For example, in the detergent market, the second ranked firm, Proctor and Gamble, with 42 per cent of the market, was able to earn profits more than four times the manufacturing industry average whereas Unilever, the market leader with 47 per cent of the market had profits less than half this amount. Similarly, in the market for electricity meters, the market leader, Sangamo (with a share of 28 per cent) earned 1.6 times the manufacturing industry average while GEC (21 per cent) earned 2.3 times the average. Oligopolistic competition between firms with similar market shares may thus mean that a market leader does not have the highest profitability but this is quite consistent with the underlying positive relationship between profitability and market share.

We observed in the previous section that even leading firms in the loose oligopoly group earned profits that, on average, were little different from the level for manufacturing industry as a whole. There was also little difference between the leaders' profits and others operating in the same market. The lack of any positive relationship between profitability and market share *within* the loose oligopoly group is brought out by equation (6) in table 2.4; the regression coefficient is not significant and the r^2 value is close to zero.[13]

MARKET SHARES AND PROFIT STABILITY[14]

We have observed that relative profit levels appear to be directly related both to market structure, broadly interpreted, and market share. To the extent that this is a reflection of the control that larger shares can have over the market we might expect the *stability* of profits to be similarly related. While all firms in a market will be subject to the same risks, firms with large shares will be better placed, on this view, to maintain their profits through their control of prices. The influence of short-term fluctuations in demand on profits, therefore, may be dampened by the ability of oligopolists to keep prices relatively stable by adjustments to output. The more competitive the market, the greater the likelihood of price and profit fluctuations.

This line of reasoning may be related to the three types of oligopoly distinguished in previous sections in the following way. We would expect the stability of profits to be greatest in the dominant firm group where the market is largely controlled by one firm. Although stability may be less in the second group due to periodic breakdowns in price coordination between the leading firms, we would nevertheless expect it to be lower than in the loose oligopoly group. Amongst *leading* firms in the three groups, therefore, we might anticipate a similar pattern to that observed for relative profit levels: profit stability will increase according to the degree of dominance exercised by one or two firms. In the case of non-market leaders two influences may be at work. Using a similar (though modified) argument to that employed by Demsetz in his discussion of profit levels, it may be that non-leaders in oligopoly, by simply following the policies of the market leader, can also insulate themselves from the worst effects of market fluctuations and as a result show similar stability in profit levels. On the other hand as they are not playing a leading role in making the decisions about how to respond, say, to a decline in demand, they may be much more vulnerable than the market leaders. If the first view is correct we would expect no difference between the profit stability of the market leaders compared with followers. In the second case, profit variability will be greater amongst non-leaders.

Table 2.5 *Relative profit stability of leading firms and others in three types of oligopoly*

Group	Number of firms	Coefficient of variation of relative profitability[a]
Dominant firms		
Market leaders	20	25.3
Concentrated oligopoly		
Market leaders	18[b]	29.4
Others	24	73.7
Loose oligopoly		
Market leaders	5[b]	29.9
Others	12[b]	60.2

[a] Coefficients expressed as percentages.
[b] One extreme observation omitted.

Using the data assembled on profit relatives and market shares we attempted to examine these relationships. For the majority of firms in the sample profit data were available for a five-year period but we also included a further ten cases where only four years were given. Twelve firms could not be included as the available profit series was for three years or less. Ideally, of course, to estimate the stability of profits a run of more than five years should be used and this limitation of the data should be borne in mind when considering the remarks that follow.

Relative profit stability was measured by calculating the coefficient of variation of profit relatives for each company in the relevant market for the five-year period. The smaller the coefficient the greater the degree of relative profit stability. As in the case of profit levels we can examine first relative profit stability of the leaders and non-leaders classified into the three oligopolistic groups described in the previous section. The values of the coefficients expressed in percentage terms are given in table 2.5.

Although stability is slightly lower for leading firms in the dominant firm group compared with those in the other two oligopoly categories there is very little difference between them, which is contrary to expectations. There may thus be no difference in the success that market leaders operating in different oligopolistic structures have in maintaining the stability of their profits. On the other hand, non-market leaders in both the concentrated and loose oligopoly groups apparently have much greater variation in their relative profitability than their respective market leaders (since data for non-market leaders in the dominant firm group are only available for two firms, they were omitted). In the concentrated oligopoly group this was about two and a half times greater and in the loose oligopoly group about twice as great. Thus, although firms with smaller shares in these groups have relative profits fairly close, on average, to the market leaders, it is nevertheless the case that, having less control of the market, they suffer wider profit fluctuations.

CONCLUSION

The Monopolies and Mergers Commission (and the Price Commission) reports are potentially a rich source of information for the analysis of market structure and performance relationships because the nature of their brief means that 'markets' and profitability are much more closely related to the theoretical concepts than is usual with published information. The main difficulty is that the timing of their reports means that few observations are available in any one year, hence our use of *relative* profitability in the present chapter. The sample is also, of course, biased towards the more concentrated markets in manufacturing industry, so all of the markets included are essentially oligopolistic.

Classifying the sample into three fairly distinctive kinds of oligopoly yielded a number of interesting results. First, amongst market leaders profits were significantly higher according to the degree of concentration: while firms with more than half of their market earned more than double the manufacturing average, those in 'loose' oligopoly earned only about 16 per cent more. Secondly, in fourteen of the twenty-one cases a non-market leader (frequently the firm ranked third by market share) had the highest profits in the market. This result, coupled with the finding that in two of the oligopolistic groups there was little difference between the relative profitability of the market leaders and others in the same market, cast some doubt, thirdly, on the Demsetz view that high profits in oligopoly are mainly the result of the efficiency of the largest firms.

The reliability of the use of the *relative* profit measure was tested using a control sample for the period 1972–4 and the regression results were sufficiently similar to those of the full sample to suggest the measure could reasonably be used. There was a significant and positive relation between market share and relative profitability for the whole sample and also for the concentrated oligopoly group alone when all firms were included. In the much smaller sample of 'dominant firms' the relationship was also positive (but just failed to be significant) and implies that such firms may retain a strong incentive for increasing their market share even when it is already in excess of 50 per cent.

Our expectations of finding a positive relation between relative profit *stability* and market share were not borne out, although ideally a longer time series of data would have been more appropriate for this analysis. One result that did emerge was that in the two less concentrated oligopoly groups the stability of relative profits was much greater for the market leaders than for others with smaller shares.

Taken together, the results highlight the complexity of the relationship between market dominance and profitability. They suggest that while some firms may owe their position to efficiency others may be using it to maintain market power. This issue is also explored in the next chapter. Whether or not leading firms in effect allow those with smaller market shares to participate in higher profits through tacit collusion (as the results in table 2.3 indicate) is discussed in chapter 4.

3

DOMINANT FIRMS IN THE TWENTIETH CENTURY

INTRODUCTION

In his article on the formation of United States Steel, Stigler (1965) mentions the well-known decline in the company's share of national output from 66 per cent at its formation in 1901 to 42 per cent by 1925. According to Worcester, in a slightly earlier paper, leading theorists had also associated the case of declining market share by a dominant firm with the cement, cans, meat-packing, and cigarette industries (Worcester, 1957, p. 338). His own paper was an attempt to provide an explanation of what he clearly regarded as a well established principle. The position was, however, far less clearcut than Worcester evidently believed for in a subsequent paper Stigler (1966) provides long-term evidence for seven American and British industries. In at least three of the United States industries and four in the United Kingdom the share of the dominant firm actually increased (see the next section for more detail). To be fair to Worcester we should add that his analysis was concerned with the case where the dominant firm behaved 'passively' because this had usually been assumed in the theory of price leadership which was his main interest. Where the dominant firm could act aggressively to maintain or improve its position, the decline could be reversed or prevented – a point appreciated by Worcester, for which he is not given sufficient credit in a recent paper by Geroski and Jacquemin (1984). In fact one purpose of Stigler's study was to measure the effect of mergers on the industrial structure of the industries concerned in order to assess the overall impact of antitrust policy. His estimates apply approximately from the opening years of the century to about 1960. In this period the United Kingdom had no merger policy while it is generally agreed that United States policy only became effective after the Celler-Kefauver Act of 1950. For most of the period, therefore, mergers were a means of maintaining market shares, as Stigler shows.

Recently there has been renewed interest in the question of whether firms that attain a dominant position in a market will be able to maintain it or whether normal competitive forces will inevitably lead to their erosion. A major supporter of the latter view, Littlechild (1981, p. 357), has recently put the case as follows: 'Entrepreneurial profits can be earned by creativity and superior foresight, by being "first in the field". However, a profitable firm is always at the mercy of rivals attempting to develop new and better products. In the absence of artificial restrictions, there is always a tendency for entrepreneurial profits to be competed away', at the same time, presumably, as their market share declines. A very similar view has recently been put by Reekie (1979, p. 24) who provides three examples of the 'tendency for firms which have gained a dominant position to lose ground relatively, if not absolutely'. The qualification seems necessary because in one of the examples the leading firm, Imperial Tobacco, with 70 per cent of the market, lost 2.5 per cent of its share in twelve years, a loss more likely to have been due to a perennial zephyr rather than to a gale of creative destruction.

As long as competition is allowed to work, supporters of this view argue that positions of dominance will tend to be eroded either directly by competing firms producing a similar product or indirectly by new products and processes which consumers regard as superior to the old. Aside from natural and patent monopolies, the only other obvious exception to this process is the dominant firm which *itself* remains alert to new ways of improving its efficiency and its products through innovation and outstanding management. According to McGee (1981, p. 321) there will therefore be 'superior firms that continue to lead their industries, either because consumers simply prefer their products or because they are able to produce the same or better products more efficiently. Less competent present competitors and would-be entrants are "excluded" only in the sense that they cannot do as good a job, which is a very poor reason to denounce those who can.'

In the absence of an aggressive acquisition policy, therefore, the market share of dominant firms would, on this view, generally be expected to decline, unless they maintain their position through their superior efficiency, in which case they should not be subject to the attention of the antitrust authorities.

In complete contrast, Williamson (1972), while prepared to accept that firms may originally gain dominant positions for a variety of reasons, including superior efficiency, and a unique innovation of management nevertheless argues that because of market failure it may subsequently be very difficult to dislodge them, even in the absence of exclusionary conduct or mergers on their part. The result is, therefore, an inferior industrial performance. (For a discussion which reaches similar conclusions but from a different perspective of 'dominance' see Geroski and Jacquemin, 1984.)

The first part of his argument rests on what he calls 'default failure'. Outstanding managerial talent is comparatively rare. Firms fortunate enough at a particular phase of their development to be blessed with such men or women are likely to grow to a position of dominance. The flair of these individuals will show itself in a number of ways (managerial practices and organisational form, for example) which will have an important influence on the firm long after they themselves have departed. 'The firm may then remain dominant despite the lack of any continuing superior acuity' (p. 1517). The general position is made worse, according to Williamson, if other firms fail to seize their own opportunities. 'The dominant firm may have displayed no special management expertise, but extant and potential rivals, on whom the responsibility for self-policing functions devolves, may have been uncommonly inept' (*ibid.*). In such circumstances, he concludes, where unassisted market processes cannot in a reasonably short period of time correct the position, some direct intervention (like antitrust policy) should be considered as a remedy.

The second aspect of what he regards as a market failure is better known and relates to chance or stochastic influences on industrial structure. This he terms 'chance event failure'. The point has been made much more familiar to British students than their American counterparts, especially through the work of Prais. Excellent expositions of the process are available (see in particular Prais, 1976, chapter 2 and Scherer, 1980, pp. 145–150) and we need only refer here to the main points. Thus if firms in an industry are initially all of the same size and have, by assumption, an equal chance of the same rate of growth but at the end of each time period some variation in their *actual* rates of growth is observed, then there will be a tendency for the size distribution of firms to become unequal. The special relevance of this process to the present discussion is that once some firms have grown to dominance they are likely to remain, because in each period they have the same chance of growth as those which have been 'unlucky' in previous periods. 'Thus, repeated application of the same stochastic mechanism that, within a relatively brief interval, gave rise in some industries to concentration, cannot reliably be expected to undo this result in any short period of time' (*ibid.* p. 1519).[1] Systematic rather than random influences may either reinforce, neutralise or outweigh the process[2] and new entry may similarly have a modifying effect, but to the extent that the process continues to work it will produce inequality in firm sizes. Furthermore, it depends in no way on the market conduct of the dominant firms concerned. The reason why they continue in their position will have nothing to do with behaviour that antitrust authorities might find objectionable. It therefore assisted Williamson in building up his case for intervention, even where no conventional antitrust abuse existed.

The final part of his argument as to why dominant positions once attained may be difficult to reverse, relates to what he sees as the special character to entry barriers in mature industries. By the time an industry reaches this stage in its development demand will have become predictable, production and marketing methods well tried and undisturbed by dramatic innovation, and, perhaps most important, producer–customer relations long established. As a result, according to Williamson, entry to such industries may be especially hard: 'Unlike entry at an early stage in an industry's development, where *differential* experience and reputation effects are, perforce, negligible, cost differences between established firms and new entrants at a mature stage are to be anticipated precisely because these factors now may be considerable' (p. 1520, emphasis added).

Furthermore, where such industries are dominated by one firm these influences are likely to be reinforced. The dominant firm will be able to administer what Williamson terms 'variety'. It is not clear what precisely the term means in the context of a mature industry where fundamental innovations no longer occur and where, presumably, the pattern of product differentiation is well established. But he argues that rivalry that might normally be expected to take place amongst changes and refinements will be absent where one firm dominates. In this case the firm can administer and assess internally the alternative possibilities and thereby avoid 'the unsettling effect of competitive market tests... Thus whereas in a fully competitive market the independently acting firm is a variety generator in relation to its rivals, the dominant firm absorbs this potential variety through internal decision making processes' (p. 1521). Why even a dominant firm should be able to settle this question without recourse to a market test is not explained. Even if it can avoid such a test it is not obvious why this should make entry even more difficult.

His final point has more force and can be illustrated from a number of examples reported by the Monopolies Commission (see, for example, Utton and Morgan, 1983, chapter 3). A potential entrant may be more reluctant to enter an industry dominated by a single firm than one where a number of firms already compete. In the former case entry will almost certainly be at the expense of the market share of the dominant firm which is likely to respond fiercely to protect its position. In a less concentrated industry where active competition among existing firms is likely to be persistent, the impact of new entry will be more dispersed.

Williamson's analysis leads him to conclude that positions of dominance, once attained, may be very difficult for normal market processes to erode. He is at pains to emphasise that such longevity may owe nothing to anticompetitive tactics on the part of the dominant firm or to horizontal mergers. He is therefore led to suggest that the American antitrust authorities should be prepared to act as a corrective force to this special case of 'market failure'.

For present purposes his contribution is of interest because of its emphasis on the permanence of large market shares, a position quite at odds with those who have argued that dominant positions inevitably decline unless rejuvenated by acquisitions or defended by unfair means. Parts of this argument are far from convincing, as critics have been quick to point out. What prevents other firms, for example, from encroaching on the market share of a dominant firm which originally owed its position to a person of unique managerial talent? If profits are abnormally high as a result of this influence, it is difficult to see why they should remain so after the genius is gone. Although the quality of talent cannot be copied, organisational innovations and even technical improvements can be. Similarly his argument that competitive sloth may leave a dominant firm in control of a market does not really stand up, especially when viewed in an international context. Posner (1976, p. 93) concludes his own critique and defence of *non*-intervention by the antitrust authorities as follows: 'In short, it takes a good deal of strained and *ad hoc* argumentation to explain persistent monopoly or concentration without assuming unlawful exclusionary practices, lawful patent protection, economies of scale, superior management, competitive pricing or other factors that would not normally justify dissolution proceedings'.

Where such a sharp dichotomy of views occurs the empirical evidence should resolve the issue. In fact at the time that both Posner and Williamson were writing, although there was by no means a complete analysis of a large sample of American industries previously characterised as 'dominant firms', there was readily available the painstaking study by Stigler (1966) of seven British and American manufacturing industries, mentioned above. Surprisingly, neither author refers to the study despite the fact that the detailed market share estimates of dominant firms and, particularly the contribution that periodic mergers made to the maintenance of their market shares, make it directly relevant to the discussion.

In the next section of this chapter we therefore discuss the Stigler study in some detail and also update the market shares of the dominant firms in the United Kingdom industries, paying particular attention to the role of acquisitions. This is followed by a discussion of a larger sample of British industries, usually characterised as dominant firm oligopolies, and we trace the changes in market shares that have occurred over the period 1935–50 to 1975–80. We then attempt to assess the role of mergers and imports in recent years on the market shares of the leading firms.

MARKET SHARES IN THE LONG RUN IN SEVEN INDUSTRIES: THE STIGLER SAMPLE

The main object of Stigler's study was not simply to record the progress of market shares of dominant firms but to determine the extent to which an active antitrust policy caused the pattern to be different from what it otherwise might have been. As he says, the task is formidable: 'A world more favourable to scholars would have had many United States, some of which had antitrust policies' (p. 259). As a substitute he compares the experience of the United States with the United Kingdom, an economy 'in which there is no public policy against concentration of control'[3] (*ibid*, p. 263).

For this purpose he was able to assemble detailed information for seven industries in the two countries: cars, cement, cigarettes, flat glass, soap, steel, and rubber tyres and tubes. The availability of adequate data was a major factor governing the coverage of the sample. Since the United States economy grew from roughly twice the size of the United Kingdom economy at the turn of the century to about four times the size by the mid-1960s, national concentration should be lower in the United States than in the United Kingdom, and declining relatively. To reduce the bias from this source regional estimates for two American industries (cement and steel) were used in the comparison between the countries.

The data showed quite clearly that concentration as measured by the Herfindahl index was considerably higher in the United Kingdom in five of the seven cases (cement, cigarettes, glass, soap and tyres) than in the United States. One of the conclusions therefore was that 'these instances are compatible with the hypothesis... that the Sherman Act was a modest deterrent to high concentration' (p. 265).

In the period covered by Stigler's analysis significant increases in concentration occurred in three industries (cars, flat glass, and soap), slight increases in two (cement and steel) and decreases in two industries (cigarettes and tyres). We have updated the concentration measure in six[4] of the industries to the middle or late 1970s. The details are given in table 3.1. In five of the six cases concentration had declined somewhat since the late 1950s and early 1960s. Even allowing for the possibility that the basis of the estimates may be slightly different from that used by Stigler (which are noted in the footnote to the table), the direction of change is unlikely to be affected. In the case of cars and flat glass the decline was clearly due to the growth of imports, while in the soap, cement and tyre industries the decline was a result of changing market shares amongst existing firms in what are all well-established oligopolistic industries. The only exception was in the cigarette industry where the Imperial Group's recovery of market share was reflected in a slight increase in the concentration index. One other interesting point about concentration changes shown in table 3.1 should be noted. The two industries which were the subject of multi-firm amalgamations around the turn of the century, cigarettes and cement,[5] had an almost identical structure three-quarters of a century later: the concentration index for cigarettes was 0.507 in 1903 and 0.508 in 1976; for cement it was 0.359 in 1900 and 0.388 by 1978. The position of the

Table 3.1. *Concentration and market shares for a sample of industries*

	Opening estimate		Closing estimate		Recent estimate	
Concentration[a] (Herfindahl index)		*Stigler study*				
Cars	0.02–0.05	(1905)	0.0253	(1964)	0.234	(1976)
Cement	0.359	(1900)	0.395	(1959)	0.388	(1978)
Cigarettes	0.507	(1903)	0.496	(1959)	0.508	(1976)
Flat glass	0.190	(1904)	0.904	(1955)	0.836	(1967)
Soap	0.057	(1900)	0.432	(1961)	0.270	(1976)
Tyres and tubes	0.363	(1924)	0.271	(1952)	0.214	(1975)
Steel	0.036	(1900)	0.065	(1960)	[d]	
Market share of the leading firm[a]		*Stigler study*				
Cars	0.305	(1924)	0.368	(1964)	0.275	(1976)
Cement	0.594	(1900)	0.598	(1959)	0.580	(1978)
Cigarettes	0.710	(1903)	0.652	(1959)	0.660	(1976)
Flat glass	0.288	(1904)	0.950	(1955)	0.910	(1967)
Soap	0.460	(1915)	0.594	(1961)	0.406[b]	(1976)
Tyres and tubes	0.584	(1924)	0.465	(1952)	0.270[c]	(1975)
Steel	n.a.		n.a.		n.a.	

Sources: Stigler, G. J. (1966), especially table 21: Bhaskar, K., *The Future of the European Car Industry*, Kogan Page, 1979; Price Commission, *The Associated Portland Cement Manufacturers Ltd – Increase in Cement Prices*, HMSO, 1978; Price Commission, *Imperial Tobacco Ltd – Cigarettes and Cigarillos*, HMSO, 1978; Price Commission, *Lever Brothers Ltd – Soaps, Detergents and Related Products*, HMSO, 1978; Fishwick, F., *Study of the Evolution of Concentration in the UK Manufacture and Supply of Tyres*, EEC Commission, 1977.

[a] Year given in brackets.

[b] Stigler interpreted the soap market broadly to include soap and detergents. The same procedure has been followed for the estimate for 1976, although Stigler's estimate was based on domestic consumption whereas the later estimate is based on sales.

[c] Estimate based on sales to the original equipment market. Dunlop was estimated to have 28 per cent of the (new) replacement market.

[d] No estimate made in view of nationalisation.

leading companies in these two instances was obviously central to the development of the industry. Their market shares are also given in table 3.1, together with those of the leaders in the other industries. (More detail is given in the appendix to this chapter.)

The pattern of the market shares of the leading firms in the small sample of industries gives us some preliminary evidence on whether dominant firms tend to decline over time. Four of the six cases support the Williamson view that dominant shares, once attained, may persist indefinitely unless strong antitrust action is taken to dismantle them. According

Table 3.2. *High and low market shares of industry leaders*[a]

	Cars	Cement	Cigarettes	Soap
Opening share	0.305	0.594	0.710	0.460
Peak	0.350 (1929)	0.750 (1912)	0.910 (1920)	0.670 (1921)
Trough	0.197 (1952)	0.580 (1928)	0.738 (1933)	0.515 (1938)
Peak	0.390 (1955)	0.700 (1938)	0.841 (1938)	0.594 (1961)
Trough	0.275 (1976)	0.549 (1981)	0.652 (1959)	0.406 (1976)
Closing share	0.18 (1983)	0.56 (1983)	0.66 (1976)	0.41 (1976)

Sources: As table 3.1.
[a] Market share (and year).

to table 3.1, the leading firm in the cement, car, cigarette and soap industries had experienced little loss of market share for a large part of this century. The most extraordinary case is Associated Portland – now called Blue Circle – which had a market share of 59 per cent after its formation in 1900 and a share of 58 per cent seventy-eight years later. The Chief Officer of the Group appears to believe that there is something almost mystical about a market share of 60 per cent. Early in 1983 when the Group was making a takeover bid for a much smaller company, Aberthaw, and when it seemed that the bid would be referred to the Monopolies Commission, he was reported as saying: 'Blue Circle's share of the market stood at 60 per cent a few years back and all that the merger would do is to take it back to the previous level' (*The Guardian*, 27 January 1983). Similarly, Imperial Tobacco's share stood at 71 per cent in 1903 and was still 66 per cent in 1976.

On its emergence as market leader in 1924 the firm that eventually became the British Motor Corporation, and subsequently BL, had a market share of 31 per cent and, despite a multitude of problems, this was still 28 per cent in 1976 (although subsequently it has had a more dramatic fall; by 1983 its share was about 18 per cent of the British market). Lever's share of the soap market was 46 per cent in 1915 and about 41 per cent in 1976. Only one case, Dunlop in the tyre market, appears to support the Posner contention that dominant firms will tend to decline in the absence of artificial impediments to entry. Its market share was more than halved from 58 per cent in 1924 to about 27 per cent in 1975. The remaining case, Pilkington, in the flat glass market, had slightly less than 30 per cent of the market in 1904 but by the mid-1950s was almost a complete monopolist and has largely retained that position despite an increase in imports.

At this stage, therefore, and given the very limited coverage of the sample, Williamson appears to win the argument. But before drawing too strong a conclusion two further aspects of the six industries can be investigated a little further. First, how *stable* have the market shares of the leading firms been, especially in the four industries where the position of the leader was apparently unchanged at the end of the period? Secondly, what role have mergers played in sustaining the share of the market leaders?

Table 3.2 shows the peaks and troughs of the market shares of the leading firms at various dates during the century.[6] All cases, not surprisingly, show considerable variation in the market shares of the leading firms: at their peak the shares were 20 percentage points or more above the lowest level. In three of the four cases the leading firm increased its market share (substantially in the cases of cigarettes and soap) after its initial emergence. The exception was APCM which had its market share practically halved in the twelve years following its formation, but a subsequent amalgamation more than restored its position. After the initial period, however, all firms saw their share eroded in a way predicted by the Worcester model. Morris Motors' share declined from a peak of 35 per cent in 1929 to under 20 per cent in 1952; APCM's share fell from 75 per cent in 1922 to 55 per cent in 1931; Imperial's share of 91 per cent had fallen to 74 per cent by 1933; Lever's share of the soap market stood at 67 per cent in 1921 but at 52 per cent in 1938. Since the early 1950s, although the changes have generally not been so dramatic as in the earlier period, the general cyclical pattern has remained: a high market share has tended to be eroded and then subsequently regained, at least in part. Imperial Tobacco illustrates this pattern most clearly, although it is also present in the other three industries. Imperial's postwar share of 82 per cent of the cigarette market fell to 56 per cent by 1964, but recovered to 66 per cent by 1976. Lever's share of the soap market was 52 per cent in 1954, 59 per cent in 1961 but fell considerably in 1976 (note the qualifications made to the estimated share of 41 per cent for 1976 in table 3.1). Probably because of the maturity of the technology in the cement industry and the successful maintenance of a cartel, APCM has reduced the variability of its market share, although even here it has moved from 67 per cent in 1955, 62 per cent in 1968 to 56 per cent early in 1983.

The changing pattern of the market shares of the leading firms, especially the abrupt increases shown in several of the industries, leads naturally to the second question: what has been the role of mergers? If large market shares are only maintained by merger, then a strengthened policy against horizontal mergers would, over time, reinforce the natural process of decay (if, of course, this reinforcement was regarded as desirable). Williamson, writing against a background of American antitrust policy with its stringent approach to mergers, has argued that dominant firms can maintain their position without the rejuvenation brought by acquisitions.

As far as our current very restricted sample is concerned, although the experience of different industries has varied, the evidence suggests that mergers have been playing a diminishing part in the progress of the market shares of leading firms as the century progressed. We must recognise, however, that this is partly due to the structure of the sample: where a dominant firm emerged fairly early on there may be little scope subsequently to acquire firms that have much effect on its market share. In his summary analysis of the contribution of mergers to *concentration* in the sample, Stigler shows that whereas mergers were frequently the major source of change up until approximately the mid-1930s, thereafter their role declined markedly.[7]

Our main concern, however, is with the market shares of the leading firms: a concentration increase may occur while the leading share remains unchanged. We have already mentioned that in two of the industries (cement and cigarettes) the leading firm was created out of a multi-firm amalgamation at the turn of the century. Since then mergers have played a key role in the increase or maintenance of the leading firms' market share; in the cement industry by the acquisition of British Portland Cement in 1912, of Red Triangle in 1931, of Alpha in 1938, and of Aberthaw in 1983. In contrast, despite Imperial's uneasy majority shareholding in Gallaher in the 1930s and 1940s (it finally sold off its interest in Gallaher in 1968), mergers have played a relatively minor part in their market share. Similarly Lever's position in the soap industry was considerably strengthened by a series of acquisitions in the first quarter of the century, but thereafter were unimportant. Dunlop's declining share of the United Kingdom tyre market has never been offset to any extent by mergers. This leaves a further two cases, flat glass and cars, where key mergers in more recent times have changed the industry structure significantly. Pilkington's key acquisition of Chance in the early 1950s is referred to below (p. 44). The 1952 merger between Austin and Morris to form BMC established the group as the market leader, after Morris' market share had declined throughout the 1930s and 1940s. Subsequently, of course, the group has acquired two other car firms (Jaguar and Rover) but only its merger with Leyland Motors in 1968 increased significantly, for a short time, its share of the market.

It would be unwise to draw any strong conclusions from our discussion of the restricted sample of industries, assembled originally for Stigler's earlier study. The main purpose has been as a preliminary exploration of the issues which we examine in more detail for a larger sample, covering a more recent period, in the next section. The discussion does indicate, however, the tenacity with which a large firm may hold on to its position in the market, despite some cyclical fluctuation in its share. In five of the six industries the leading firm has retained that position for more than 50 years and, judging by the conclusions of bodies like the Monopolies and Mergers Commission, has managed this without the kinds of anti-competitive practices often associated with large firms but infrequently found to have much substance.

LONG-RUN MARKET SHARES OF DOMINANT FIRMS IN UNITED KINGDOM INDUSTRY

In order to extend the analysis of the previous section we assembled a sample of nineteen markets, known for the dominance of a particular firm, and traced the market share of the leader over a period of at least 22 years and frequently much longer. As before, we are especially concerned to discover whether or not dominant market shares tend to decline or whether they can be maintained in the long run in the face of changed production conditions and the variable intensity of competition.

Tracing market shares for a sizeable number of companies over a long period is extremely difficult, not least because of the problem of ensuring that the 'market' is defined consistently. For this reason we started with the dominant firm sample of markets used in chapter 2, supplemented in some cases from the 'concentrated oligopoly' sample and Stigler's sample. The leader in each of the markets eventually included in the sample had to have a market share of 50 per cent or more in the opening year which was determined largely by the availability of reliable information on market shares, and varied from a year just prior to the Second World War to one as near to the end of the war as possible. The closing year was meant to be in the middle to late 1970s, but in some cases an earlier year had to be taken where the more recent market share estimate was judged unreliable. We then examined the progress of the market leaders' shares over the whole period.

A potentially important source of bias in this procedure needs to be recognised. As the core of the sample was based on a relatively recent Monopolies and Mergers Commission (or Price Commission) report this obviously means that it includes mainly markets *currently* dominated by a particular firm. Markets which in a previous period may have been similarly dominated but where the leading firm has had its position eroded are less likely to appear in the sample. In this way, therefore, the sample is likely to be unrepresentative of markets where a dominant firm has declined dramatically. On the other hand the MMC can be asked to investigate a market where one firm has a share of as little as one quarter and a number of these cases were included in the 'concentrated oligopoly' sample (see appendix, chapter 2). The market leaders in this sample had recent market shares ranging from 28 to 52 per cent but in only one case (detergents) was it probable that the firm had had 50 per cent or more of the market at the time of the Second World War. Hence although some bias is likely in the sample it may not be very great. Also firms having a very large market share in the opening year could have declined considerably but still have retained, by the mid-1970s, a market share large enough to interest the MMC.

Table 3.3 contains the market shares for the opening and closing years for the nineteen companies in the sample. As the number of years involved differs considerably between markets it is not possible to make precise comparisons but it is feasible to look at the broad changes that have occurred. If we use the benchmark that a significant change in market share is where that of the market leader has risen or declined by 10 percentage points or more, then it is clear from the table that an increase occurred in five cases and a decrease in eleven, with three cases remaining (approximately) unchanged. If the sample also tends to be biased against market share declines, for the reason given above, the importance of significant falls in the market shares of dominant firms is underlined. Seven of the declines in market shares affected firms that were some way from being 'monopolies' in the opening year: thus, for example, the Blue Circle Group's share of the cement market fell from 70 per cent to 56 per cent, wallpaper manufacture from 71 per cent to 53 per cent, CPC's share of the starch market from 50 per cent to 34 per cent, Turner and Newall's asbestos share from 51 per cent to 35 per cent, Shell Mex and BP's share from 51 to 35 per cent, Dunlop's share of the tyre market from 57 per cent to 28 per cent and Unilever's share of the soap market from 53 per cent to 28 per cent. In four cases the shares of what could be regarded as near monopolists were substantially reduced; that is, in matches (from 90+ per cent to 57 per cent),[8] in cigarettes (from 84 per cent to 66 per cent), in industrial gases (from 98 per cent to 75 per cent) and in open top cans (from 100 per cent to 75 per cent). The only dominant firm to retain a market share of 80 per cent or above throughout the period was in safety glass.

Two other points can be made about those markets where the leading firm's position had been eroded. First, despite the decline in market share from an initial position of 50 per cent or more, the original leader retained that position in every case. Thus, even where the relative decline has been substantial, it has not been great enough (at least for our rather restricted sample) to topple the market leader. All the companies mentioned in table 3.3 retain their 'dominance' of the market to this extent. For this reason Williamson might argue that his analysis remains substantially correct, even though a majority of cases in the sample show declining market shares. Secondly, however, it is also true that in most of the eleven cases

Table 3.3. *Long-run changes in the market shares of dominant firms*

		Market share				Percentage point change	Length of period (years)
Product group	Company	Opening share (%)	Year	Closing share (%)	Year		
Matches[a]	Wilkinson-Match	90+	1935	57	1973	−33	38
Tyres	Dunlop	57	1935	28	1975	−29	40
Soap	Unilever	53	1938	28	1976	−25	38
Open top cans	Metal Box	100	1939	75	1976	−25	37
Industrial gases	BOC	98	1953	75	1978	−23	25
Wallpaper	Reed	71	1937	52–3	1977	−18	40
Cigarettes	Imperial Group	84	1938	66	1976	−18	38
Asbestos	Turner and Newall	60+	1945	43	1971	−17	26
Starch	CPC (UK) Ltd	50	1938	34	1977	−16	39
Petrol	Shell Mex & BP	51	1953	35	1975	−16	22
Cement	Blue Circle	70	1938	56	1982	−14	44
Detergents	Unilever	54	1938	49	1976	−5	38
Safety glass	Triplex (Pilkingtons)	85–90	1951	85	1980	—	29
Breakfast cereal	Kelloggs	51	1950	54	1976	+3	26
Flat glass	Pilkingtons	58	1935	77	1980	+19	45
Clutches	Automotive Products	70+	1938	90	1976	+20	38
Plasterboard	BPB	70–75	1951	100	1978	+25	27
Cellulosic fibre	Courtaulds	60	1938	89	1966	+29	28
Contraceptives	LRC Products	50	1939	90+	1982	+40	43

Source: Details of the sources of the market share estimates are given in appendix 2 to this chapter.

[a] This treats Swedish Match's market share as independent from that of the British Match Corporation, but see p. 49 below.

the scope for oligopolistic rivalry has increased as the leader's share has declined. The degree of competition in, for example, the markets for matches, cigarettes, wallpaper, starch, asbestos, petrol distribution, tyres and toilet soap has probably intensified over the last 30 years or so, even if the form of that competition has not always been of a kind that yields immediate benefits to the consumer.

One way in which it would be possible to test the hypothesis that a decline in the share of the market leader had led to an improved (allocative) performance of the industries concerned would be to compare the relative profits of the firms at the beginning and end of the period. If their profits had tended to regress towards the mean this would indicate that, *ceteris paribus*, intensified competition, as shown by the decline in their market shares, was having the predicted effect. Unfortunately, as we explained in chapter 2, while it is possible to derive relative profit figures for most dominant firms in the sample, defined in an appropriate way, the data are only available for a limited number of years, usually the period immediately preceding a report of the MMC or Price Commission. A comparison of profits for industries of different structure and for periods some years apart cannot therefore at present be made. Attempts to test this hypothesis with different samples of American industries led to some heated discussion but to results which unfortunately were ambiguous, apparently owing a great deal to the method of sampling and even interpretation of the results. Using the same data MacAvoy *et al.* (1971) and Brozen (1971) were able to come to diametrically opposing conclusions, the former asserting that industries with high and stable concentration levels were able to keep their profits (at least for a decade) above the 'normal' level, while the latter maintained that there were clear indications that high profits tended to regress to the mean over time.

What does emerge from the British sample of dominant firms is that, in those cases where the leading firm had either increased or maintained its market share, relative profitability was considerably higher than in markets where the leading firm had suffered a decline. Thus the average profit relative (as defined and used in chapter 2) for nine firms whose share had declined was 1.18, that is, 18 per cent above the manufacturing industry average, while for seven firms with an unchanged or increased market share the figure was 2.17 – profits were more than twice the average.[9] In view of the direct relationship between market share and profitability established in chapter 2 these results could perhaps have been expected. (The mean market share of firms in the first group was 55 per cent while that of the second group was 78 per cent). But it is consistent with the hypothesis that a decline in the market share of the dominant firm does indicate an intensification of competition and an erosion of their profitability.

In those cases where the dominant firm market share increased over the observed period, the change was dramatic, ranging from 22 percentage points in flat glass to 40 percentage points in contraceptives. Where such large gains had been made in an earlier period it was often the case, as we observed in the previous section, that a large part of the change could be attributed to acquisitions. We explore the extent to which this was also true for firms in the present sample in the following section.

In his analysis of the long-run market power of dominant firms in the United States, Shepherd (1983) concluded, first, that the rate of erosion had declined in the period 1948–73, compared with the earlier period 1910–35, which would accord with the Williamson view, but also, in comparison with the United Kingdom, positions of dominance in the United States were older and more firmly established. The samples are different, his interpretation of an 'industry' is much wider than our approximation to a 'market', and he is looking at market power rather than the share of the leading firm but, nevertheless, the results in table 3.3 give added support to this conclusion that on the whole dominant market shares in the United Kingdom are vulnerable.

Compared, therefore, with the preliminary discussion of the previous section and based on the limited sample of six industries, the more broadly based sample for the later period tends, if anything, to support the Posner–Worcester analysis of dominance rather than the Williamson analysis, especially if the sample is biased somewhat against markets with declining market shares by the leading firms.

The results in table 3.3 can also be interpreted in terms of Schumpeterian innovation and change. As industries develop at different rates and are subject to shocks of one kind and another at different time periods, the forces that were shaping the market shares of the dominant firms in the opening year would have varied in intensity across markets. In some, the very success of the leading firm may already have begun to undermine its future, in the way that Posner and others suggest. In other cases the observed opening market share may reflect concentration by increasing forces which were gaining momentum. It is therefore practically impossible to predict with any accuracy the market shares, even for dominant firms, for more than a few years in advance. From the vantage point of the 1930s it could not have been foreseen, for example, that Dunlop's share of the tyre market, Unilever's share of the soap market and CPC's share of the starch market would decline considerably over the next 30 years or so while, from approximately the same position, Pilkington in flat glass, LRC products in contraceptives and Courtaulds in cellulosic fibres would do exactly the opposite.

The fact that large market shares are subject in the long run to considerable variation, with a strong likelihood of decline, raises an interesting point for policy. Periodically it is suggested that dominant firms resistant to market forces should be broken up in order to increase competition and thereby improve the performance of the industry. A proposal along these lines has recently been made for the United States, for example, by Williamson, in certain specified instances. After a long period of abstention from such drastic antitrust remedies the United States Department of Justice recently reached an agreement with the giant A.T. and T. Corporation whereby the latter is to sell off approximately half of its total assets after an action that lasted almost eight years.[10] There are at least three reasons for expecting such remedies to be comparatively inefficient. First there are what can be termed the impact costs of dismantling a going concern which, even if the enterprise had previously been organised as a series of semi-autonomous divisions, are likely to be considerable. Secondly, certain economies of size may have to be sacrificed, especially in the important area of product development and innovation. Thirdly, once the deed is done it may take a considerable time before the separate components of what was previously one enterprise actively compete in the market and produce the superior performance that the policy anticipated. In view of these problems the 'remedy' provided by the market may be preferable, despite the evident delays involved, especially if Demsetz (1973) is correct that large firms which retain a leading market position do so only as long as they remain efficient and innovative although, as we saw in chapter 2, there is some evidence that he may have overstated the case.[11]

MERGERS, IMPORTS AND DECLINING MARKET SHARES

In his analysis of why the market shares of dominant firms decline Worcester (1957) explained that the trend could be reversed if the firms took on an aggressive role in their pricing policy or if they were able to acquire some of their growing rivals. For at least five of the companies mentioned in table 3.3 the earlier reports of the MMC contained some strong criticism on these grounds. The British Match Corporation and British Oxygen were criticised for, in effect, using predatory pricing through undisclosed subsidiaries (although that term was not actually used). Wallpaper Manufacturers was seen as systematically acquiring competitors whenever they looked like challenging the leader's position. Similarly the Commission was sceptical of the benefits to the public of Imperial Tobacco having a large minority shareholding in its leading rival, and of Courtaulds' continued forward integration by merger into the textile and clothing industries. Despite these policies however, in four of the five cases table 3.3 shows that the market share of the leading firm declined substantially.

On the other hand, if dominant firms attempt to abuse their position, competition from imports may hasten their decline. A domestic firm may be able to acquire a home based competitor or, failing this, reach a (tacit) understanding on market shares more easily than with companies located overseas, although the growth of multinational enterprises may often tend to make the relationship more complex.

In this section, therefore, we look more closely at the markets listed in table 3.3 and try to determine first, the role of mergers in increasing or maintaining a position of dominance and, secondly, the extent to which the growth of imports has served recently to weaken the position of the market leaders.

Table 3.3 shows eight markets where the share of the leading firm was unchanged or increased in the period reviewed. Acquisitions appear to have played an important part in four of those cases: flat glass, safety glass, plasterboard and man-made fibres. In the other cases their role was negligible. In the flat glass industry when Pilkingtons finally acquired Chance Brothers in 1951 after a long period of cooperation and voluntary sale over the years of Chance shares to Pilkington, this was 'the only major merger in the history of the trade' (see Walshe, 1974, p. 85) leaving Pilkingtons without any domestic competitors. Although the way the merger was accomplished shows it not to have been of the aggressive kind to maintain market share, it remains true, as Walshe points out, that Chance was worth more to Pilkingtons because of the additional discretion over prices it allowed, than to the only other possible purchaser which would have been a foreign company.

In the safety glass market two key acquisitions by Pilkingtons also had the effect of eliminating effective competition from domestic producers although in this case competition from imports has meant that an initial increase in market share has been eroded. By the end of the period the leader's market share was approximately the same as in 1951 although in this case ownership had changed. Until its final absorption by Pilkingtons in 1965 the market leader had been Triplex Safety Glass, although the two companies had collaborated closely at least since 1926 when Pilkingtons became its main supplier of raw glass and particularly from 1929 onwards when the two companies jointly founded a safety glass subsidiary, Triplex (Northern) (see Monopolies Commission, 1968a, pp. 24–5). By 1951 the only effective domestic competition to Triplex was from British Indestructo Glass (BIG) which was then owned by four motor manufacturers and which accounted for 10–15 per cent of the United Kingdom market 'while practically all of the remaining 85 to 90 per cent went to Triplex' (*ibid* p. 28). Pilkingtons, which had been steadily building up its holding in Triplex, had acquired by 1965 a holding of more than 50 per cent and so in effect became the market leader with something less than 90 per cent of the market. When Triplex acquired BIG in 1967 under an arrangement with the two remaining owners, Ford and British Motor Holdings, their control of United Kingdom production was practically complete. (The Monopolies Commission report shows, however, that some very small safety glass manufacturers remained in 1966 (p. 46).) Thus, although Triplex's original dominant position was not due to merger, it was used subsequently (by Pilkingtons) to dispose of competition, albeit by agreement rather than by a takeover bid.

A rather similar stance towards some significant acquisitions was taken by BPB (formerly British Plasterboard) in the plasterboard industry. Horizontal acquisitions which turned it into a complete monopoly, were 'thrust upon it' rather than as a result of the company, the undisputed market leader, positively seeking them out. Although on the surface this was undoubtedly the case, the underlying reason for at least some of the acquisitions was probably the vertical strength of BPB and the problems its competitors faced in securing independent raw material supplies (Monopolies Commission, 1974, chapter 2). In the late 1930s, for example, BPB acquired a dozen smaller firms and their gypsum mines mainly to ensure that it did not have to depend on imports for its essential raw materials (para. 16). By the end of the war it was responsible for most of the gypsum and gypsum plaster produced in the United Kingdom (as well as being the largest producer of plasterboard). Three subsequent acquisitions in the 1950s and 1960s eliminated all remaining domestic competition, although in no case did BPB take the initiative. The acquisitions were as follows: Plaster Products (Greenhithe) in 1955; Bellrock Gypsum Industries in 1967 with a market share of 11 per cent; and ICI plasterboard plant in 1968 with a market share of about 11.5 per cent. Thus effectively all of the increase in market share by BPB shown in table 3.3 was a direct result of acquisitions.[12]

Our main concern is with horizontal market shares and so in the remaining case where the leader's position has been strengthened by merger, Courtaulds in cellulosic fibres, we concentrate on its acquisitions in this market over the period 1957–63, even though the Monopolies Commission laid particular emphasis in its conclusions on Courtaulds' spate of vertical acquisitions in the textile and clothing industries.[13] The acquisition of five smaller fibre producers in this period probably accounts for about half of the increase in market share shown in table 3.3. But in the specialised acetate section of the market the impact of merger was much more important: Courtaulds' acquisition of the leading producer, British Celanese, in 1957 increased its share of United Kingdom production capacity from about 24 per cent to 97 per cent (Monopolies Commission, 1968b, p. 103). The Monopolies Commission considered, rather ambiguously, that while 'Courtaulds does not appear to have gone out of its way to acquire competitors', nevertheless 'we do not consider that it was inevitable that Courtaulds should become the sole producer of viscose and almost the sole producer of acetate, nor that it should have such a large share of the total supply of the market' (*ibid*, p. 62). In one of its most strongly worded conclusions the Commission recommended (amongst other things) that any further proposed acquisitions by Courtaulds in the textile and clothing industries should first be cleared by the Board of Trade.[14]

In all cases, therefore, the leaders' already established position of dominance in the market allowed them to mop up remaining domestic competitors in a non-aggressive way, and often through the initiative of the acquired firm. Although some of the important mergers in these markets occurred after the 1965 Monopolies and Mergers Act, for example, it is significant that none of them was referred to the Monopolies and Mergers Commission.[15]

In addition to those dominant firms which enhanced their position by some well-timed acquisitions there were others which attempted such a strategy but failed. We have already mentioned briefly the case of Wallpaper Manufacturers (WPM) which fairly continuously since its foundation at the turn of the century through an amalgamation of 31 companies, had acquired any rival which looked like gaining a significant market share. The Monopolies Commission regarded these activities, not surprisingly, as designed to preserve WPM's monopoly and recommended that the company should in future gain clearance from the Board of Trade before attempting to make any further acquisitions in the market.[16] Just prior to the Commission's enquiries WPM had acquired its two leading rivals (Smith and Walton, and KL Holdings) which together accounted for about 20 per cent of the market. The acquisitions raised WPM's share to about 80 per cent, rather more than it had enjoyed in 1951 (Hart *et al.*, 1973), but there were rapid indications that, as in previous decades, the share would not be maintained. Several companies, including ICI and the paint-makers Berger, Jenson and Nicholson, entered the industry and developed vinyl coated papers which WPM was slow to follow. In 1965 WPM itself was taken over by the Reed papermaking group, but this did not prevent its market share from declining once more, as table 3.3 shows. In fact the most recent decline and the growth of ICI to a market share of about one quarter (MINTEL, January 1979) has changed the industry into a duopoly rather than a monopoly. If the market were to be classified now (rather than at the time of the Monopolies Commission report, as in chapter 2) it would fall in the 'concentrated oligopoly' rather than the 'dominant firm' group.

Without going into detail, a rather similar history has occurred in the cigarette, cement, and tyre markets with the leading firm periodically attempting to regain a lost market share by strategic acquisition, only to see the process recur, usually after a time lag.

Before looking at the effect of imports in the nineteen markets in more detail, it is important to remember that the Monopolies and Mergers Commission, when investigating dominant firms, always examines the 'availability of supplies' to the United Kingdom, that is, sales in the United Kingdom, from whatever source, and not merely the 'sales' of United Kingdom producers.[17] It also usually establishes any direct links there may be between leading British producers and imports (as in the cases of Courtaulds and CPC in the starch market). Thus the market shares in table 3.3 are in this respect a much closer reflection of the underlying structure of the market than is usually available.

A number of the markets in the sample had already been included in part of an earlier study which was directly concerned with imports (Utton and Morgan, 1983, especially chapter 3) and we were able to draw on those results in what follows. Of the nineteen cases, imports provided a significant (that is, greater than 10 per cent) share of the market in only five cases; starch, tyres, flat glass, cellulosic fibres and matches. According to the Monopolies Commission report, imports of starch had always taken a significant portion of the total market, even allowing for those directly made by the market leaders. By 1975 imports (including those made by CPC) accounted for about 30 per cent of the market. In another market where the leader's position had been substantially eroded, tyres, imports accounted for about 18 per cent of the market by 1975. Although there was some evidence that a small proportion of these were made through a Dunlop subsidiary, the majority were from other manufacturers (*ibid.* p. 26). In the other two cases imports have potentially a key role in that they provide the only competition to the monopoly supplier within the United Kingdom. Since the Commission report on flat glass in the 1960s, imports have grown significantly. According to that report they represented about 10 per cent of United Kingdom sales in 1966 but by 1980 the share was approximately 23 per cent.[18] Whether this is higher or lower than would have been the case had Pilkingtons faced more competition from other domestic producers is difficult to say, given the general growth in international trade that has taken place since the Monopolies Commission report. But clearly Pilkingtons' discretion over prices is more circumscribed than its dominance of United Kingdom *production* might suggest.

In its recommendations in the report on the supply of cellulosic fibres, the Monopolies Commission, which was highly critical of Courtaulds' supply policy to its domestic customers, saw import competition as a potentially important source of restraint on Courtaulds' exercise of market power. At the time of the report the constraint was potential rather than actual because Courtaulds was not only protected by a very high tariff but had taken a series of steps to ensure that imports were kept to a minimum and also that those that did arrive in the United Kingdom were in effect 'regulated' by Courtaulds 'for the purpose of preserving its monopoly of supply' (Monopolies Commission, 1968b, para. 223).

They concluded that the arrangements that Courtaulds made with foreign companies (within EFTA) exporting to the United Kingdom were to remove a threat to its prices and profits. The company had estimated that imports from Scandinavia were already costing it about £200,000 a year in profits and that this might rise to £1–1½ million (Monopolies Commission, 1968b p. 81). According to other overseas fibre producers they had refrained from undercutting Courtaulds in the United Kingdom for fear of retaliation in their own domestic markets and in other markets where they were in competition with Courtaulds. In addition British fibre *users* claimed that the reduction of duties within EFTA had not brought about increased competition in the United Kingdom, partly because of Courtaulds' 'arrangements' with Swedish and Austrian producers, partly because the Norwegian producer supplied wood pulp to Courtaulds and would not compete in the United Kingdom, and partly because the Finnish producer had agreed to limit exports to the United Kingdom in exchange for know-how from Courtaulds. Prices from the Swedish producer (Svenska Rayon) had previously been below those of Courtaulds but rose after Courtaulds acquired an interest in the company and distributed Svenska's products in Britain. It was also alleged that some of Courtaulds' British customers were unwilling to buy imported fibres because they feared that Courtaulds might cut their supplies (*ibid.*, p. 123).

Although in some cases the assertions of competitors or customers may reflect their own inability to come to terms with competition in an industry, there was more than enough evidence that Courtaulds had taken a number of steps deliberately to impede competition from imports, rather than defeat it in the market. Not surprisingly, therefore, a major emphasis of the Commission's recommendations was on the freeing of international competition so as to provide an effective counterweight to Courtaulds' dominant position in the British market. They therefore recommended: (i) a substantial reduction in import duties on cellulosic fibres, (ii) an ending of those arrangements with other EFTA producers which restricted competition in the supply of cellulosic fibres in the United Kingdom, (iii) a prohibition on any further arrangements by Courtaulds with other foreign fibre producers, after the import duties had been reduced, and (iv) a review by the Board of Trade twelve months after the reduction of import duties, to discover whether its purpose had been achieved (*ibid.*, p. 87).[19]

In the event, the Board of Trade, after a lag of fifteen months during which it received Courtaulds' reaction to the Commission's conclusions, decided not to implement the central recommendation on tariff reduction. Although Courtaulds agreed to end its special arrangements with other EFTA producers, this was probably of limited importance beside the tariff proposal.[20] The central question, therefore, is what has happened to imports since the Commission's report? At the time of the report imports amounted to just under 9 per cent of total British supplies and we estimated that the figure had grown to just under 13 per cent by 1979[21] which, given the general growth in world trade since the middle 1960s is very modest. Nevertheless, imports probably provide a more significant independent market share in the United Kingdom than has been available since the Courtaulds acquisitions of the late 1950s and early 1960s, even though the strong protectionist tendencies of the Common Market continue to make themselves felt through the multi-fibre agreement.

Finally, in the United Kingdom market for matches the second largest market share in 1973, when the Monopolies Commission reported on the proposed merger between the British Match Corporation (BMC) and Wilkinson Sword, was held by Swedish Match (SM) and amounted to 28 per cent of the total.[22] Here again, however, there is considerable ambiguity about the nature of SM's market share. The two companies have had a long association. Technical and commercial links remained strong in 1973 and SM still had a one-third shareholding in BMC which dated from 1927. The Monopolies Commission mentioned that all of SM's products 'are sold in the United Kingdom (*in competition with BMC products*) through J. John Masters (Holdings) Limited, a BMC subsidiary' (Monopolies Commission, 1973, p. 3, italics added). It did not, however, comment on whether, as a result, the competition was more apparent than real. Yet given the relationship of the companies, BMC's control of imports might be regarded as greater, for example, than those of Courtaulds in the fibre market. In its earlier report on the market for matches, at a time when the two companies also maintained a number of restrictive agreements, the Monopolies Commission had included SM's share with BMC's rather than treat them independently.[23] If this is a more accurate reflection of the realities of competition in the British match market, then BMC's share in table 3.3 would be about 85 per cent (with imports accounting for the bulk of the remainder) rather than 57 per cent, and their true share would thus have remained relatively unchanged since 1951. In the absence of more detailed analysis of precisely how SM's products are sold 'in competition with' BMC's, however, it is difficult to determine which treatment is the more accurate.[24]

The cases mentioned so far are those where imports form a significant fraction of domestic sales but there are three other markets in the sample where imports play some part: safety glass, contraceptives and breakfast cereals. By the mid-1970s imports amounted to about 7–10 per cent of all

British sales in these markets (Utton and Morgan, 1983, chapter 3 and Monopolies and Mergers Commission, 1975) and for the first two, provided the only effective competition to the dominant domestic producer. The position of Triplex (Pilkingtons) in safety glass has been discussed above (p. 44). In the contraceptive market LRC Products has twice been referred to the Monopolies Commission within a decade, twice been condemned for charging too high prices and earning excessive profits.[25] But on neither occasion was there evidence that the dominant company had deliberately attempted to restrict or regulate imports in the way, for example, that Courtaulds had. Although some of the forms that competition had for a time taken in the retail market were criticised by the Commission (Monopolies Commission, 1968b, para. 54), in the end it was hard put to discover why such a profitable industry had not been entered by other (large) domestic firms or why imports which formerly had accounted for a much larger share were now comparatively insignificant.

Other domestic producers are a much more important source of competition in the breakfast cereals market than imports. In this respect the market is much more like the remaining cases in table 3.3, where the pattern has been largely one of increased competition from other British firms tending to erode the share of the dominant firm (despite in some cases mergers to bolster their position).[26]

CONCLUSION

Examination of the long-term record of the market shares of dominant firms should help to resolve the issue of whether the forces of dissolution, as Worcester argued, are stronger than those of reinforcement anticipated by Williamson. The discussions in the second to the fourth section in this chapter have illustrated, not surprisingly, that the pattern is a very complex one.

According to the record of six industries which Stigler traced out for a period of about 50 years, positions of dominance, once attained, can persist, especially if they are bolstered by strategic mergers (as in cement, flat glass and cars). It was also noticeable, however, that leading market shares are subject to quite violent fluctuations with firms gaining or losing 10–15 percentage points in as many years (table 3.2).

The experience of the larger sample over the last 30–40 years discussed in the third and fourth sections was very varied. But given that eleven of the nineteen cases showed the dominant firm suffering a significant decline in market share (and that the number may be biased downwards), it is hard to resist the conclusion that over this period the forces of erosion have been rather stronger than those of reinforcement. We should not make too much of this conclusion, however, since in every case the dominant firm retained its position at the head of the market and in all but five cases still held, at the end of the period, a share of 50 per cent or more.

Although mergers were an important source of market share increase in some significant instances in the larger sample (safety glass, cellulosic fibres, plasterboard), there were equally cases of large increases without mergers (contraceptives, clutches) as well as market share losses despite mergers (wallpaper, and from the earlier sample, cars).

Considering the recent growth of world trade it was somewhat surprising that imports only accounted for a significant share of the British market in five cases, although the source of much of the market share data (the MMC) may have tended to bias the number downwards since there is a stronger probability that markets insulated from foreign competition will be referred to the MMC than others. In two of these cases (cellulosic fibres and matches) some ambiguity surrounded the precise role of imports: in particular whether they were genuinely in competition with the leading firms' output in view of the association between them and importing companies.

On the whole the evidence of this chapter is sufficiently varied to suggest that both Williamson and Worcester are correct to some extent and that both therefore should win prizes. There are sufficient examples both of dominant firms losing their pre-eminence and of others consolidating theirs (while showing an unacceptable performance) to make the policy implications more subtle than either Williamson or Posner have suggested. We take up this issue in more detail in the concluding chapter.

4

COMBINED MARKET SHARES AND PRICE COLLUSION

INTRODUCTION

An unresolved controversy in industrial economics has concerned the pricing behaviour of firms operating in highly concentrated markets. One view, generally associated with the work of Bain, who built on the theory of oligopoly developed by Chamberlin, is that firms in such markets will realise the mutual advantage of collusion. Assuming that their position rests, at least in part, on barriers to entry, they will therefore be able jointly to enjoy a monopoly or near monopoly profit. If the law only allows tacit rather than overt collusion, an agreed policy on prices and related conditions may be difficult to administer and police. On the whole, the fewer the number of firms the easier the monitoring procedures would be and hence the more successful the policy. One inference that was frequently made from this line of reasoning was, therefore, that collusion and concentration would go together: the more concentrated the industry, the easier the supervision and the more stable the price structure. As a result the performance of such industries would be suboptimal.

More recently, however, a number of writers have challenged these conclusions, particularly since they appear to rest on the over-simplification that oligopolistic firms will find it relatively easy to sink their differences in arriving at a collusive price structure. In a highly influential article Stigler (1964) pointed out that even where there were comparatively few sellers, although their task may be easier than the multi-firm case, they will still find it difficult to avoid periodic attempts to chisel and renege on the agreement. Although high concentration may, therefore, be a necessary condition for successful collusion it is not a sufficient condition. Posner demonstrates succinctly the difference between the two views when he writes: 'There is nothing in the theory of cartels to suggest that if there are just a few major sellers in a market competition will automatically disappear. Each seller must still decide whether to limit output, and this implies at least tacit agreement with his major competitors. The problems of arriving at a mutually agreeable price and then maintaining it in the face of temptations to cheat exist whether few or many sellers are trying to collude' (Posner, 1976, p. 54). Other conditions will be necessary for successful collusion.

The central feature that distinguishes the two approaches, therefore, is the degree of active competition likely in concentrated oligopolies. If the leading sellers have to pursue a positive and independent price policy there may be no reason for their *joint* share of the market to change over time. The corollary of this, according to Posner, is that a 'long-term decline in the market shares of leading firms.... is a symptom of price fixing, though an ambiguous one since it may be attributable to other factors' (p. 68). One of the latter, presumably, may be that large market shares breed inefficiency and therefore make the firms vulnerable to new competition, although this is more likely to be the case when accompanied by collusion.

The main purpose of this chapter, therefore, is to examine this hypothesis in the light of the recent experience of the United Kingdom manufacturing sector. If the joint share of the leading firms in heavily concentrated industries decreases through time by an amount significantly greater than might normally be expected this would suggest that they had been colluding, although individual cases may yield a different explanation. Alternatively if the joint share only changed by a 'normal' amount this could be taken as indirect evidence of the effectiveness of competition even in oligopoly. The results must be treated cautiously, however, because an unchanged concentration ratio can disguise considerable variation in the actual market shares, and even the identity, of leading sellers.

To isolate cases of high concentration we use the criterion that the five-firm concentration ratio in the opening year must have been at least 75 per cent. The markets included should, therefore, be rather similar to those referred to in chapter 2 as 'concentrated oligopolies'.

CONCENTRATION CHANGES IN OLIGOPOLY

To examine the question in detail we can make use of the series of concentration in United Kingdom manufacturing industry prepared by the Business Statistics Office (1979) and recently extended in another National Institute study (Utton and Morgan, 1983). In that study concentration data for the period 1958 to 1977 were used for a sample of 121 products where adjustments were also made to allow for imports. The same sample is used in the present chapter. Since most commentators are now agreed that a major competitive influence in many United Kingdom markets comes from imports, to use concentration data without attempting to include imports may have given misleading results. (The results using the concentration series unadjusted for imports is given in the appendix to this chapter.) We therefore analyse the trend of adjusted concentration for the period 1958 to 1977 paying particular attention to products where the opening year share in sales of the five largest firms was 75 per cent or more.

Table 4.1 *Simple regressions of adjusted product concentration for various years on adjusted concentration in 1958, for a sample of 119 products*[a]

Time period	Constant[b]	Regression coefficient	r^2	Mean adjusted concentration % Year	Mean
				1958	52.6
1958–63	6.500 (1.499)	0.924 (0.026)	0.917	1963	55.1
1958–68	13.744 (2.134)	0.850 (0.037)	0.822	1968	58.5
1958–75	19.865 (2.579)	0.690 (0.044)	0.676	1975	56.2
1958–77	20.714 (2.693)	0.644 (0.046)	0.625	1977	54.6

Source: Estimate from Utton and Morgan (1983), appendix table 2A3.

[a] Two products were omitted from the original sample: polishes for which no data were available for 1958 and synthetic rubber, very little of which was made in the UK in 1958 giving an unduly low 1958 concentration level.

[b] Standard errors in brackets.

As Prais (1958) and others have emphasised, in such an exercise we have carefully to distinguish 'normal' regressive tendencies from other special influences. In the case of the present sample (details of which can be found in Utton and Morgan, 1983, chapter 2 and appendix 2A3), the information in table 4.1 shows that if the opening year is compared with successive later years, for which information is available, there is simultaneously an increase in concentration and regression towards the mean. The former point is shown by the increase in the mean concentration ratios for successive periods (although the mean concentration level reached a peak in 1968, and fell back thereafter), the latter by the regression coefficients of less than unity in each case. The longer the time period considered, not surprisingly, the greater the departure of the regression coefficient from one, as products initially at the extremes of the concentration profile move, on average, towards the mean.

Since our main concern is with the 28 products which in 1958 were extreme, in the sense of having concentration ratios of 75 per cent or above, to observe the progress of concentration for these products through successive years is likely, on average, mainly to reflect the influence of regression. Thus average concentration for this group declined from 86.4 per cent in 1958 to 75.6 per cent by 1977, whereas for the whole sample

Table 4.2 *Actual and predicted levels of concentration in several years for 28 heavily concentrated products in 1958, and average concentration for the full sample*

	Five firm, mean concentration (%)		
	Heavily concentrated products in 1958 (28)		
End year	Actual	Predicted	Full sample (119)
1958	86.4	—	52.6
1963	86.2	86.3	55.1
1968	86.0	87.2	58.5
1975	78.1	79.5	56.2
1977	75.6	76.4	54.6

Source: Estimated from table 4.1.

average concentration increased by 2 percentage points from 52.6 to 54.6 per cent (see table 4.2 below). In order to estimate how much of the concentration decline was due to regression and how much was due to other influences, including collusion, we therefore proceeded as follows. The regression equations in table 4.1 can be used to predict for each period the average closing level of concentration from any given opening level. But in addition, a slight modification to the equations in table 4.1 can be used to predict the amount of concentration *change* that has been due to regression.[1] For the sample of heavily concentrated products we can then compare the observed concentration level at different years with the predicted level. The results are shown in table 4.2.[2]

The estimates are based on the assumption of *linear* regression (that is, the largest firms have the same tendency to regress as those only marginally above the mean, and as those much below mean size). In practice strongly increasing (or decreasing) returns to scale may mean that the largest firms show a lesser (or greater) tendency to regress to the mean.

For the group of 28 heavily concentrated products in 1958 we would expect, on this basis, their average concentration to have declined to 76.4 per cent by 1977. The left-hand column gives the mean concentration ratio actually observed for the concentrated product group. Over the whole period concentration declined by 10.8 percentage points, with twenty of the products showing a reduction in concentration, seven an increase and one remaining unchanged.[3] The second column gives the predicted average level of concentration for the group on the basis of the regression estimates in table 4.1. In each case the average concentration level observed was below the predicted level but the differences remained slight. By 1977, for example, more than 90 per cent of the concentration decline could be 'explained' by the normal process of regression.

The contrast with a similar analysis for the United States is striking. For various periods within the 25 years from 1947 to 1972 Brozen (1982, table 10.5, p. 295) shows that in all but one case the predicted levels of concentration in the United States for a similar sample of products were *below* the observed levels, the reverse of the position for the United Kingdom. In other words, the actual level of concentration was higher than the levels expected on the basis of the normal process of regression. Only for the whole 25-year period (1947–72) which he included in his analysis was the actual level below the predicted level. The divergence between the predicted and observed concentration levels for the British data by the mid-1970s, therefore, raises the possibility that attempted collusion amongst market leaders caused a larger than expected decline in the combined market share but given the modest differences shown in table 4.2 the suggestion must be tentative.

Brozen supplemented his comparison between predicted and observed concentration levels for heavily concentrated industries with an examination of the trend in the number of firms, on the grounds that declining concentration occurring simultaneously with an increase in the number of firms operating in a market might again signify collusion by the leaders, resulting in new entry. In such cases the market leaders might have decided to charge high short-run prices in the knowledge that this would, over time, cause an erosion of their market shares. The alternative strategy associated particularly with Bain would be to 'limit' short-run prices so as to forestall entry and maintain the joint share of the leading group. If successful, the result would be stable concentration and a more or less unchanged population of firms.

When he examined the experience of a sample of heavily concentrated American manufacturing industries, however, Brozen found an equal division between those which had an increase and those a decrease in the number of firms. There was also little association between the direction of change in concentration and changes in the number of firms. He concluded that this supported the previous result that there was little evidence of collusion amongst the leaders in such industries. For the United Kingdom sample, data on enterprise numbers in separate product groups are less readily available but we have been able to derive estimates of whether numbers increased or decreased over the period 1958–77 for fifteen of the 28 product groups in the heavily concentrated sample (see appendix 2 to this chapter). Numbers of enterprises in each group in 1977 were made available by the Business Statistics Office in the table recording seller concentration.[4] The figures for 1958 were derived from the individual

Table 4.3 *Concentration (adjusted) and enterprise changes in fifteen product groups, 1958–77*

Product Group	Concentration 1958	Concentration 1977	Direction of change in the number of enterprises 1958–1977	Number of domestic enterprises 1977
Condensed milk	89.2	83.9	D	6
Vegetables, quick frozen	79.9	70.1	I	27
Soups	85.4	60.9	D	19
Margarine	87.2	93.5	D	7
Compound fat	82.5	86.5	D	12
Ball and other bearings	88.4	61.8	D	19
Line apparatus	85.6	92.3	D	12
Gramophone records	97.8	68.1	U	12
Tractors	95.1	87.3	D	11
Finished thread	84.9	84.3	D	26
Electrical ware of porcelain	75.7	70.6	I	17
Illuminating glassware	82.7	75.7	D	9
Safety glass	97.6	84.0	D	16
Cement	84.9	92.8	D	10
Wallpaper	90.9	72.8	I	21

Sources: As for table 4.1 and appendix to this chapter.
Note: D = decrease; I = increase; U = unchanged; fuller details given in the appendix to this chapter.

reports of the 1958 Census of Production. Table 4.3 contains the information on the concentration change and the direction of change in the number of firms for the fifteen product groups over the period 1958–77.

The most frequent occurrence was of a decline both in concentration and number of firms (particularly if we include in this category two borderline cases either where concentration remained unchanged while the number of firms declined – finished thread – or the reverse – gramophone records). Eight product groups then fall into this category which runs counter to the usual hypothesis that concentration decline will be accompanied by an *increase* in the number of enterprises, signifying an increase in competition. Brozen, who found a similar effect for United States industry, suggested that the possible explanation might be that market leaders yield part of their market share to middle ranking firms already operating in the industry (see Brozen, 1982, p. 302). The market leaders may previously have held prices high enough to encourage these firms to expand to achieve additional economies of scale, without prices being high enough to shield the smallest firms in the industry. This explanation would be in line with that suggested by Worcester (1957) which we referred to above (chapter 1).

Although this may have occurred in some British industries a more important part of the explanation may be the effects of mergers and imports. It is generally agreed that the period under review witnessed an almost unparalleled volume of merger activity with important effects for the structure of manufacturing industry. The impact of this is reflected in table 4.3 where eleven of the fifteen product groups had a decline in numbers (seven of the eight which we have already mentioned above and four cases where concentration increased rather than decreased). Similarly, an important source of the decline in concentration has been the growth of imports. If it were possible to record the total number of enterprises that supplied the United Kingdom rather than simply the number of British producers, the third column of table 4.3 may have looked rather different. In other words the concentration declines shown in the table, to the extent that they are attributable to import growth, are really a reflection of an *increase* in the number of firms operating in the market.[5] The suggestion that the growth of imports has intensified competition in these markets is supported by Shepherd (1982) in his recent analysis of the experience of the United States. To the eight cases already mentioned, we can add the three (frozen vegetables, electrical ware of porcelain and wallpaper) that experienced a decline in concentration with an increase in the number of (domestic) firms and to which, therefore, the same conclusion applies. This leaves four products (margarine, compound fat, line apparatus and cement) which had an increase in concentration and a decline in the number of domestic firms. Since they are also largely free from import competition they probably conform most closely to the view that associates concentration and collusion.[6]

CONCLUSION

In this chapter our main concern has been with the joint market shares of the leading firms in oligopolistic industries rather than the individual firm shares which is the focus in other parts of the study. Using concentration data for the five largest firms, adjusted for imports, we tested the hypothesis that, *ceteris paribus*, a large combined market share will assist leaders in their *attempts* at collusion to maintain relatively high prices, but over time their efforts will tend to be undermined by competition from other firms and new entrants. A partial measure of attempted collusion was taken to be a more rapid decline in the combined market share of the leading firms than might be expected from the normal process of linear regression towards the mean. In other words, attempts at collusion to raise prices lead to a more rapid erosion of market share. Non-colluding oligopolists, by pricing according to prevailing competitive conditions are better placed to maintain market share.

In the event, the difference between observed levels of concentration and those predicted on the basis of 'normal' linear regression were so slight as to give only the most tentative support for the collusion hypothesis. Although the observed concentration levels for the sample of heavily concentrated products was always below the level 'expected', the differences were small enough to suggest that about 90 per cent of the recorded concentration declines were due to regression.

5

SUMMARY AND CONCLUSIONS

The importance of market shares in the analysis of competition has long been recognised and its comparative neglect in empirical research is explained by the difficulty of assembling suitable data. As a substitute the level of market concentration has been used, although it is acknowledged that much information about the relative strengths of the leading sellers is thus hidden. In contrast the Monopolies and Mergers Commission (MMC) in its inquiries into the conduct and performance of dominant firms has, as the present study demonstrates, paid a great deal of attention to market shares and their changes over time. In these inquiries the problem of deciding which products should be included in a market and which lie outside it is largely avoided by the terms of reference which usually state the precise product to be investigated, although as part of its overall assessment the MMC frequently has to decide which products are in effective competition with each other.[1]

Previous empirical research in the United States appeared to establish a strong link between market share and profitability which, when coupled with a much wider set of results linking market concentration with profits, looked for a time in the late 1960s and early 1970s as though it was to have a dramatic effect on policy. One proposal, the Concentrated Industries Act, was for certain oligopolistic firms to have their market shares reduced to no more than 12 per cent unless substantial losses in scale economies would result.[2] In contrast the recent review of British monopoly and merger policy[3] made scarcely any reference to market shares, and its recommendations on, for example, a change of emphasis in merger policy were very mild.

A major aim of the present study, therefore, was to underline the significance of market shares and to show how data already available could be used to test a number of hypotheses concerning the relationship between shares and market conduct and performance. Cautious use of data from many MMC and Price Commission reports allowed us to examine first the association between profitability and market shares. In the business literature there are widespread references to market share as central to profitability (see in particular Buzzell *et al.*, 1975). As we showed in chapter 2 this emphasis is well founded. Not only was there a well defined and significant relationship between profitability and market shares overall, but for leading firms in three types of oligopoly there was a significant increase in relative profitability, on average, the larger their market share. Thus dominant firms with more than half of the market were able to earn more than twice the manufacturing industry average whereas the less concentrated or 'loose' oligopolies could manage only about 16 per cent more.

The analysis of three different kinds of oligopolistic structure and the effect on profit performance is also important for another reason. Because we were using individual market shares it was possible to distinguish clearly dominant firm, concentrated oligopoly and loose oligopoly markets. Had we been using concentration ratios showing, for example, the *combined* sales of the leading five firms, most of the distinctions between the different oligopoly types would have been lost and many of the markets would have appeared in the same concentration category even though their real market structures were different and likely to yield a distinct performance. Thus a number of products which had five firm concentration ratios of 75 per cent or more in 1977, and which in many studies would therefore fall in the most concentrated category, could in the present study be more appropriately classified as 'loose oligopoly' (for example, bread and ready-mixed concrete) or 'concentrated' oligopoly (for example biscuits, flour, ice cream, detergents, cat and dog food and concrete roofing tiles), categories quite distinct from that designated as 'dominant firm' oligopoly. The inability to get 'inside' concentration ratios in this way may account for the relative lack of success that cross-section multivariate analysis of structure–performance relationships has so far had.

We were also able, in chapter 2, to throw a little more light on a controversy that has received considerable attention recently, namely whether market leaders owe their position to efficiency or to the use of market power. The fact that, in fourteen of the twenty-one markets for which sufficient data were available, firms ranked below the first earned higher relative profits than the leaders, gave some indication that the latter were not necessarily the most efficient, although we need to remember that profitability may be a rather imperfect measure for this purpose. In addition the small differences in relative profitability observed between market leaders and market followers in each of two of the oligopoly groups suggested some degree of tacit collusion on prices. Otherwise, for example, we should have seen a much closer correspondence between relative profit levels of the followers in the two groups than was actually the case.

On the other hand, a clear advantage that market leaders do have over their rivals is in profit stability. Although there was no evidence of any difference between the profit stability of market leaders in the two oligopoly groups, when compared with that of market followers an important difference emerged. For market followers profit variability was likely, on average, to be more than twice as great, a reflection probably of their far smaller degree of control over prices and especially price changes than that wielded by market leaders. Since both of the groups observed were oligopolistic, the role of smaller competitors may often be that of passive follower of changes made by the market leader, rather than initiator of changes which in timing and extent would be more to their own advantage.

The analysis of chapter 2 was essentially short-run and confined to observations usually spread over five years. In contrast, in chapter 3 we attempted to trace the progress of dominant firms over the long period, initially for a small sample developed by Stigler over the first half of the century, and then for a larger sample over a period of twenty years or more. To underline the different hypotheses that have been proposed concerning the long-run progress of market shares, we contrasted the views of Williamson on the one hand and of Posner and Worcester on the other. In contrast with many writers on the subject, Williamson argued that, for a number of reasons, markets may often fail to dislodge a dominant firm once it is established and that in such cases rather dramatic policy measures may be appropriate, such as the break-up of large firms, even though they may not in any active sense have been infringing the antitrust laws. The more conventional view as elaborated by Posner and analysed for certain oligopoly cases by Worcester, has been that positions of dominance in a particular market will usually be eroded over time by the normal processes of competition and innovation. Exceptions may occur where the firm actively responds to market share erosion either by acquiring its major rivals, a path now blocked certainly in the United States and probably in the United Kingdom by antitrust or competition policies, or by strictly controlling its internal efficiency and limiting prices below short-run profit maximising levels and thus restraining existing rivals and deterring new entrants. Far from market failure, such authors view the latter outcome as the effective working of competition.

Not surprisingly when so many conflicting factors are at work, the evidence on long-run market shares is mixed. In the sample of six markets covering a large part of the century, the shares of the leading firms in four cases showed remarkable consistency: shares created in the opening years of the century were, within a few percentage points, the same 60 or 70 years later (chapter 3, table 3.1), although in each case there was also evidence of considerable variation in the intervening years. On the other hand, the larger sample of nineteen markets covering the last 30 to 40 years suggested much more strongly that dominant firms' market shares tend to decline, even in the face (for most of the period) of a largely permissive merger policy. Thus eleven of the firms which had market shares of 50 per cent or more in the opening year had suffered a significant decline by the end of the period, while five had increased their share and the other three had maintained their position. The source of the data and the way the sample was constructed probably meant that cases of large market share reductions were *under*-represented and this tends to reinforce the main conclusion. Although lack of data meant that we could not compare relative profits at the beginning and end of the period, it was the case that firms which had increased or maintained their market shares had substantially higher profits, on average, than those whose market share had been declining, a result consistent with those in chapter 2.

To this extent, therefore, the evidence from the larger sample and for the more recent period is closer to the conventional view of dominant share decline. It may also be contrasted with Shepherd's conclusion for the United States that the *rate* of decline has diminished considerably since the Second World War. Although a direct comparison is not possible, the evidence from chapter 3 does not support such a conclusion for the United Kingdom. We should not lose sight of the additional point, however, that despite the declines in market share and the probable intensification of oligopolistic competition that this entailed, the leaders not only retained their position at the head of the market but in most cases (that is, seven of the eleven where the leading share declined) kept 50 per cent or more of the market.

When the source of market share changes was examined in more detail we found that in four of the eight cases where a dominant position had been strengthened or maintained, mergers had played a significant part (flat glass, safety glass, plasterboard and man-made fibres) although in each case the acquiring company had played a fairly passive role rather than aggressively seeking to strengthen their horizontal position. The conclusion for merger policy (which we take up below) is, however, not as clear-cut as it may seem because in the sample there was an equal number of cases where strategically timed acquisitions failed to halt a declining market share (wallpaper, cigarettes, cement and tyres).

The most important conclusion to emerge from an examination of the five cases where imports accounted for a significant fraction of United Kingdom sales was the need for detailed information about the real competitive influence of imports. The valuable role that the MMC can play in this respect was well illustrated in the markets discussed. Thus, for example, their reports showed that in three of the cases, starch, cellulosic fibres and matches, a significant portion of all imports was either made directly by the market leader or was closely regulated by them through their association with the importing companies. As we mentioned in a previous study (Utton and Morgan, 1983), the lack of systematic evidence of this kind makes it extremely difficult to analyse correctly the competitive impact of the growth of imports on many United Kingdom industries.

One conclusion from chapter 2 was that the data on relative profitability in two types of oligopoly suggested that a degree of tacit collusion allowed market followers in the concentrated oligopoly group to earn profits close to those of the market leaders. This point was considered further in chapter 4. Using a large sample of markets in manufacturing industry for the period 1958–77, we examined whether the highly concentrated markets showed greater decline in concentration than might be expected from the normal process of regression. If collusion was effective in such markets then we anticipated a greater than normal reduction in concentration as other firms sought to take advantage of the abnormal returns. A normal reduction in concentration would have been interpreted as signifying the lack of effective collusion. The main test was carried out using product concentration data adjusted for imports. The main conclusion to emerge from this analysis was that the concentration reduction amongst the most heavily concentrated products was greater than predicted by normal regression. The inference about tacit collusion may thus hold when tested with the data that takes account of all sources of supplies in the United Kingdom (including imports) rather than simply sales by British producers. It is in sharp contrast to results obtained by Brozen for the United States but is in line with a previous result (Utton and Morgan, 1983) that the more heavily concentrated markets in the United Kingdom may, through their pricing policies, have been particularly vulnerable to increased import penetration when world trade was growing rapidly.

The analysis of data from the large number of MMC reports included in this study demonstrates the key importance of market shares. In particular the rate at which these shares change over time may be central to our understanding of market conduct and performance. Data on concentration which have frequently been used in effect as a proxy for market shares may conceal more than they reveal about the actual effects of competition amongst the leaders in oligopolistic markets. As is well known, the Statistics of Trade Act precludes the Business Statistics Office from publishing information about individual firms, consequently systematic data for a large cross-section of markets cannot be made available. However, in view of the importance of market shares in oligopoly to competition policy, it would be worthwhile for the BSO, in consultation with the Office of Fair Trading, to devise indices of market share changes which would retain confidentiality but also improve on the published information currently available. The studies reviewed in chapter 1 used a variety of indices of market share instability, many of which depended on full knowledge of individual firms' market shares in different years. It is not difficult, however, to construct measures that are easily calculated and understood and yet could be freely published. An example is the simple correlation coefficient between market shares of firms at the beginning and end of the period under review. Since particular importance attaches to the shares of the leaders, the index could be separately calculated for, say, the largest five, ten and fifteen firms in a market. Information on firm sales is now kept at the BSO in a form which allows individual firms to be identified at various years for the purpose of calculation. An index of this kind, used in conjunction with other structural indicators such as the concentration ratio and number of firms in a market (which are already available), would then give a much fuller description of market structure and one which came close to the proposal by Fellner (1955) made more than thirty years ago.

For the reasons given in chapter 3, the dismantling of dominant firms which are considered to have abused their position is neither a feasible nor an efficient remedy. In fact the evidence in that chapter on the long-run erosion of large market shares in almost two-thirds of the cases studied gives some encouragement for the view that normal market processes will often provide a more effective solution. The fact, however, that dominant firms can earn persistent abnormal returns (chapter 2), and that in a significant minority of cases can bolster their position by mergers and measures designed to weaken the competitive effect of imports (chapter 3) underlines the need for a vigorous competition policy. In this respect the challenge to horizontal mergers which would substantially increase the market share of already dominant firms should be maintained. It would thus be clear in advance to all concerned that such merger proposals would be referred to the MMC (although, of course, this does not rule out the possibility that the Commission might recommend in favour of certain mergers). In addition, where a dominant firm intends to acquire a comparatively modest rival but where this would lead to the effective elimination of all or nearly all remaining domestic competitors, reference to the MMC should be more or less automatic, even though the dominant firm may not have initiated the merger plan. The major exception to this rule would be where the small rival was clearly failing and where, as a result, merger would provide a more efficient solution than liquidation. With hindsight, it might have been more appropriate if the MMC had been allowed to examine the full implications of Triplex (Pilkington's) acquisition of BIG in 1967 and of BPB's acquisition of Bellrock in the same year. Had BPB *not* acquired Bellrock it might then have been possible to form a viable competitor to BPB by a merger between Bellrock and ICI's plasterboard interests which it disposed of in the following year. As it was, by this time no other independent plasterboard producer remained so there was little alternative for the Board of Trade but to sanction BPB's purchase.

The fact that the decline of the market shares of dominant firms may take a considerable time while still leaving them at the head of the market makes it especially important to ensure that recommendations by the

MMC for maintaining or increasing competition should be carried out in full and subsequently monitored. In the past this has not always been the case in such markets: for example, the Imperial Group did not have to dispose of its holding in Gallaher (although subsequently it did so), Courtaulds continued to make vertical acquisitions, tariff reductions were not made on cellulosic fibres and colour film. In view of the impossibility, since Britain's membership of the EEC, of unilateral tariff reductions as an instrument of competition policy, other recommendations, especially those concerning imports, should be made effective.

An additional source of restraint on the market power of dominant firms should come from the large buyers that a number of them face. In theory the countervailing power that a monopsonist can bring to bear on a single seller or group acting together may ensure prices well below the monopoly level. In practice, where the sole buyer is a nationalised industry or Government department, some recent examples suggest that such power may be more apparent than real. Hoffmann-La Roche eventually paid back about £4 million the the National Health Service and reduced its prices after the MMC had concluded that it had abused its dominant position in the tranquiliser market. BICC and other manufacturers of telecommunications cable paid back £9 million to the Post Office after the discovery by the MMC of an undisclosed (and unregistered) market sharing agreement. It has been argued in the Press *The Guardian*, 3 February 1984) that BOC supplies to the National Health Service of oxygen equipment are on terms unduly favourable to the company. Similarly, it has been alleged that LRC has been able to maintain its monopoly supply of surgical gloves to the National Health Service because of inordinately long delays by the Department of Health and Social Security in granting the necessary licences to a foreign company which wished to supply gloves at a lower price (*The Observer*, 1 April 1984).

Part of the problem is undoubtedly that, whereas a large customer in the private sector can always threaten to start production itself if it does not get satisfactory terms from a dominant seller, this threat is not usually credible for a government department or a nationalised industry. But in many cases a much more potent policy would be to call for tenders from overseas companies and make it clear that, in markets where there is effectively only one domestic producer, a policy of 'buying British' which most departments and nationalised industries are under strong political pressure to pursue, will not necessarily apply. A consistent policy of this kind would also help to maintain the correct 'arms-length' commercial relationships between officials in the buying departments and those in the supplying company.[4]

By these means and the natural erosion of dominant shares through market forces adverse consequences could be minimised without resort to the more drastic remedy of the kind suggested by Shepherd (1975). Against the background of American experience he recommended the introduction of a progressive tax on market shares above a certain level. Although he argued that such a policy would not affect efficiency but simply give dominant firms an incentive to reduce their market shares in whatever way they thought appropriate, the evidence on market shares, efficiency and profitability is certainly not strong enough to support this contention, especially for the United Kingdom. The policy suggestions discussed above on the other hand have the added advantage that they can be implemented within the present framework of competition policy merely by a change of emphasis.

APPENDIX 2.1

MARKET LEADERS

Dominant firm markets: leading market share ⩾ 50 per cent, next largest less than half the size

Market	Firm	Market share (%)	Average ROCE	Average profit relative	Years covered
Breakfast cereal	Kelloggs	57.1	46.1	3.81	1967–71
Matches	BMC	57.0	17.6	1.31	1969–73
Diazo copying materials	Ozalid	53.0	33.6	2.80	1972–5
Indirect electro-static repro. equipt.	Rank Xerox	95.7	35.9	2.48	1971–5
Primary batteries:					
zinc carbon	Ever-Ready	74.5	21.8	1.72	1968–72
Mercury	Mallory	69.5	32.6	2.57	1968–72
Open top cans	Metal Box	78.5	21.4	1.74	1964–8
General line cans	Metal Box	50.0	14.4	1.17	1964–8
Wire rope	British Ropes	49.9	9.9	0.68	1967–71
Flat glass	Pilkingtons	91.0	22.7	1.76	1961–5
Safety glass	Triplex Pilkingtons	77.7	34.4	2.75	1962–6
Cement	APCM	60.5	7.3	0.46	1973–7
Plasterboard	British Gypsum	100	14.5	1.20	1967–71
Contraceptive sheaths	LRC	90.0	101.3	7.56	1969–73
Clutch mechanisms	Automotive Prods.	62.6	28.6	2.33	1963–7
Cigarettes	Imp Tobacco	66.3	23.6	1.50	1974–7
Industrial gases	BOC	75.0	14.4	0.93	1975–8
Colour film	Kodak	76.8	48.2	3.57	1960–4
Librium & valium	Hoffmann La Roche	99.0	70.0	6.19	1970
Wallpaper	WPM	74.7	16.3	1.19	1960–2
Cigarette filter rods	Cigarette components	85.4	44.5	3.62	1963–7
Cellulosic fibre	Courtaulds	90.7	17.2	1.41	1964–7

Concentrated oligopoly: top 2 with 50 per cent or more of the market (but not in first group) or first with 50 per cent and second firm *more than* half the size.

Market	Firm	Market share %	Average ROCE	Average profit relative	Years covered
Flour	RHM	31.2	22.8	1.57	1971–5
Ice cream	Unilever	37.0	22.2	1.43	1972–6
Household detergent	Unilever	47.5	24.9	1.93	1961–5
Footwear machinery	BUSM	45.5	17.4	1.43	1967–71
Meters	Sangamo	28.1	25.4	1.61	1973–7
Glucose	B & Polson	43.5	22.7	1.91	1966–70
Winding wires	BICC	41.1	4.6	0.30	1972–6
Electric lamps	BLI (Thorn)	42.0	12.1	1.03	1965–7
Building bricks	London Brick	40.0	23.8	1.70	1970–4
Ceramic sanitary ware	Armitage Shanks	30.9	20.8	1.34	1972–6
Concrete roofing tiles	Redland	42.6	43.1	2.99	1976–80
Glass bottles	Rockware Group	28.2	14.7	0.95	1972–6
Asbestos goods	Turner & Newall	44.0	15.0	1.24	1965–9
Cat & dog food	Pedigree Petfoods	50.3	46.7	3.11	1972–5
Rolls for rolling mills	British Rollmakers	52.2	9.5	0.79	1969–71
Telecommunications cable	BICC	28.4	26.8	1.73	1972–6
Biscuits	United Biscuits	40.0	35.8	2.27	1977–8
Savoury snack foods	United Biscuits	30.0	24.9	1.58	1977–8
Supertension cable	BICC	45.8	11.8	0.76	1972–6
Domestic gas appliances	Thorn	34.7	23.9	1.51	1974–8
Fibre cordage	British ropes	49.4	12.1	1.00	1967–71

Loose oligopoly: top two with less than 50 per cent of market

Market	Firm	Market share %	Average ROCE	Average profit relative	Years covered
Bread	RHM	24.2	4.6	0.32	1971–5
General winding cable	BICC	32.3	18.0	1.16	1972–6
Ready mixed concrete	RMC (UK)	34.4	38.9	2.54	1975–9
Petrol (whole-sale)	Shell	19.4	2.4	0.15	1976–8
Starches	B & Polson	26.1	25.0	2.10	1966–70
Frozen food	Birds Eye (Unilever)	33.5	18.0	1.22	1971–4
Pottery	Royal Doulton Tableware	15.4	17.1	1.06	1976–8
Beer	Bass	20.0	16.3	1.01	1976–8
Mains cable	BICC	29.4	13.2	0.85	1972–6

NON-MARKET LEADERS

Market	Firm	Market share %	Average ROCE	Average profit relative	Years covered
Dominant firm markets					
Cement	Rugby Portland	15.0	27.3	1.73	1973–7
Industrial gases	Air Products	20.0	24.9	1.60	1974–8
Concentrated oligopoly					
Flour	ABF	19.4	42.8	2.95	1971–5
	Spillers	26.8	22.8	1.57	1971–5
Ice cream	Glacier	28.8	16.8	1.08	1972–6
Detergents	P & G	42.2	54.3	4.21	1961–5
Meters	Landis & Gyr	27.1	9.2	0.58	1973–7
	Ferranti	24.2	4.6	0.29	1973–7
	GEC	20.6	36.8	2.33	1973–7
Winding wires	AEI	32.0	12.8	0.83	1972–6
	Pirelli General	7.9	2.4	0.15	1972–6
	Delta	5.3	1.2	0.08	1972–6

Market	Firm	Market share %	Average ROCE	Average profit relative	Years covered
Electric lamps	Philips	24.0	19.1	1.63	1965–7
	Osram (GEC)	20.5	19.3	1.65	1965–7
Ceramic sanitary ware	Twyfords	20.7	18.2	1.17	1972–6
	Ideal Standard	18.5	27.0	1.74	1972–6
	Doulton	16.7	8.6	0.55	1972–6
Concrete roofing tiles	Marley Tile	23.4	20.1	1.40	1976–80
	Sandtoft Tileries	8.1	53.5	3.72	1976–80
	Anchor Building Prods	3.8	14.3	0.99	1976–80
Glass bottles	United Glass	27.0	19.3	1.25	1972–6
	Redfearn Nat Glass	16.5	20.4	1.32	1972–6
Cat and dog food	Spillers	30.1	19.2	1.28	1972–5
Rolls for rolling mills	Davy Int	33.6	16.7	1.39	1969–71
Domestic gas appliances	TI	19.8	−5.1	−0.33	1974–8
	Cannon	9.3	14.5	0.95	1975–9
	UGI	7.9	16.6	1.06	1974–8
Loose oligopoly					
Bread	ABF	19.9	−1.1	−0.08	1971–5
	Spillers	15.3	−11.8	−0.81	1971–5
General wiring cable	Delta	12.0	22.8	1.47	1972–6
	Pirelli General	6.9	13.8	0.89	1972–6
	AEI	6.6	25.6	1.65	1972–6
Ready mixed concrete	Amey Roadstone	13.2	24.4	1.55	1976–9
	Pioneer Concrete	9.7	44.6	2.92	1975–9
	Tilcon	5.6	29.0	1.90	1975–9
	Steetley Const	4.1	22.4	1.46	1975–9
	Topmix	3.8	10.5	0.69	1975–9
	Tarmac Roadstone	2.7	4.3	0.28	1975–9
	Redland Readymix	3.0	18.3	1.20	1975–9
Petrol	BP	14.7	0.3	0.02	1976–8
	Esso	19.0	11.9	0.73	1976–8
Frozen foods	Ross Foods	12.4	5.8	0.37	1972–4
	Findus	11.3	7.3	0.47	1972 4
Beer	Whitbread	13.0	10.2	0.65	1974–8
Savoury snack foods	Nabisco Brands	17.0	21.0	1.39	1977–81

Note: ROCE = Rate of return on capital employed.

APPENDIX 2.2

RATIO OF NET INCOME TO AVERAGE NET ASSETS FOR COMPANIES IN MANUFACTURING INDUSTRY

Year	Spliced series	Year	Spliced series
1960	15.7	1970	11.3
1961	13.4	1971	12.3
1962	12.1	1972	14.4
1963	12.9	1973	16.6
1964	13.5	1974	15.5
1965	12.7	1975	13.6
1966	11.2	1976	17.2
1967	11.3	1977	16.3
1968	13.0	1978	15.2
1969	12.5	1979	14.2
		1980	8.9

Calculated from: Business Monitor – Company Finance (MA3) 11th Issue (Table 11) and 13th Issue (Table 12).

Changes in the series

1960–4: coverage includes all public and former private non-exempt companies engaged in manufacturing with net assets £0.5 million or gross income of £50,000 or more in 1960.

1964–9: same criteria used for all companies meeting the assets/income figures in 1964.

1969–74: coverage includes companies with net assets of £2 million or more, or income of £200,000 or more in 1968. (Changes involved net assets of only 1.5 percent.)

1974–80: coverage includes companies with net assets of £5 million or more and gross income of £50,000 or more in 1973.

APPENDIX 2.3

PROFITABILITY, MARKET SHARE AND OVERALL SIZE

A view which has frequently been expressed, but which has so far found very little support, is that the very large diversified firm gains certain pecuniary advantages which allow it, on average, to earn abnormally high returns. For example, the costs of such firms may be lower because they can raise capital more cheaply or buy inputs at lower prices and this puts them at an advantage over smaller firms. In markets where they are well established,[1] they can thus earn high profits, *ceteris paribus*. Independent of market share, therefore, overall size of firm would, on this view, have a separate and direct effect on profitability. In a similar vein, a number of writers have argued that in markets with heavily differentiated products, the entry barriers created by advertising and sales promotion will also tend to keep profits above average for the leading firms (see Dalton and Levin, 1977, and Shepherd, 1975).

In order to test these relationships we again used the control sample of 40 markets referred to above, all of which related to the period 1972–4. Overall size of firm was measured by capital employed for the whole group taken from *The Times 1000*, 1973–4. Since data on advertising expenditures were not systematically available at this level of aggregation, to approximate the degree of product differentiation, we relied on a dummy variable which took the value of 0 for producer goods and 1 for consumer goods. In the event, neither of the additional variables proved significant. Both had the wrong (negative) sign and their standard errors were as big or bigger than the coefficient estimates. Market share, however, retained its significant and positive influence on relative profits.[2] In contrast with these results, both Shepherd, and Dalton and Levin, generally found a significant relationship between profit rates and product differentiation measured by the advertising–sales ratio. But when the latter authors tried a dummy variable to represent the product differentiation effect the result was not significant. A more precise measure of product differentiation may, therefore, have given a more positive result for the British data. In the case of overall firm size both previous studies recorded no significant positive relationship with profitability (although in some of the Dalton and Levin tests a significant *negative* relationship was found). In the present study with narrowly defined and distinct markets, in addition to the non-significant regression result, the simple correlation between relative market profitability and overall firm size was −0.056. Taken together with other evidence, all of this suggests that perhaps the 'conglomerate size' hypothesis should at last be laid to rest.

APPENDIX 2.4

SOURCES

MARKET LEADERS

Dominant firms

Monopolies Commission – *Breakfast Cereals*, HMSO, 1973.

Monopolies Commission – *British Match Corporation and Wilkinson Sword Ltd*, Report on the Proposed Merger, HMSO, 1973.

Monopolies and Mergers Commission – *Diazo Copying Materials*, HMSO, 1977.

Monopolies and Mergers Commission – *Indirect Electrostatic Reprographic Equipment*, HMSO, 1976.

Monopolies and Mergers Commission – *Primary Batteries*, HMSO, 1974.

Monopolies Commission – *Metal Containers*, HMSO, 1970.

Monopolies Commission – *Wire and Fibre Ropes*, HMSO, 1973.

Monopolies Commission – *Flat Glass*, HMSO, 1968.

Price Commission – *Associated Portland Cement Manufacturers Ltd – Increase in Cement Prices*, HMSO, 1978.

Monopolies Commission – *Plasterboard*, HMSO, 1974.

Monopolies and Mergers Commission – *Contraceptive Sheaths*, HMSO, 1975.

Monopolies Commission – *Clutch Mechanisms for Road Vehicles*, HMSO, 1968.

Price Commission – *Imperial Tobacco Ltd – Cigarettes and Cigarillos*, HMSO, 1978.

Price Commission – BOC Ltd – *Compressed Permanent Gases and Dissolved Acetylene Sold in Cylinders, Cylinder Rentals and Fixed Charges*, HMSO, 1979.

Monopolies Commission – *Colour Film*, HMSO, 1966.

Monopolies Commission – *Chlordiazepoxide and Diazepam*, HMSO, 1973.

Monopolies Commission – *Report on the Supply of Wallpaper*, HMSO, 1964.

Monopolies Commission – *Cigarette Filter Rods*, HMSO, 1969.

Monopolies Commission – *Man-made Cellulosic Fibre*, HMSO, 1968.

Concentrated oligopoly

Monopolies and Mergers Commission – *Flour and Bread*, HMSO, 1977.

Monopolies and Mergers Commission – *Ice Cream and Water Ices*, HMSO, 1979.

Monopolies Commission – *Household Detergents*, HMSO, 1966.

Monopolies Commission – *Footwear Machinery*, HMSO, 1973.

Monopolies and Mergers Commission – *Starch, Glucoses and Modified Starches*, HMSO, 1971.

Monopolies and Mergers Commission – *Insulated Electric Wires and Cables*, HMSO, 1979.

Monopolies Commission – *Electric Lamps*, HMSO, 1968.

Monopolies and Mergers Commission – *Building Bricks*, HMSO, 1976.

Monopolies and Mergers Commission – *Ceramic Sanitaryware*, HMSO, 1978.
Monopolies and Mergers Commission – *Concrete Roofing Tiles*, HMSO, 1981.
Monopolies and Mergers Commission – *Rockware Group Ltd, United Glass Ltd, Redfearn National Glass Ltd, Report on the Proposed Mergers*, HMSO, 1978.
Monopolies Commission – *Asbestos and Certain Asbestos Products*, HMSO, 1973.
Monopolies and Mergers Commission – *Cat and Dog Foods*, HMSO, 1977.
Monopolies and Mergers Commission – *Davy International Ltd and The British Rollermakers Corporation Ltd, Report on the Proposed Merger*, HMSO, 1974.
Price Commission – United Biscuits (UK) Ltd – *Biscuits, Crisps, Nuts and Savoury Snacks*, HMSO, 1979.
Monopolies and Mergers Commission – *Domestic Gas Appliances*, HMSO, 1980.
Monopolies Commission – *Wire and Fibre Ropes*, HMSO, 1973.

Loose oligopoly

Monopolies and Mergers Commission – *Flour and Bread*, HMSO, 1977.
Monopolies and Mergers Commission – *Insulated Electric Wires and Cables*, HMSO, 1979.
Monopolies and Mergers Commission – *Ready Mixed Concrete*, HMSO, 1981.
Price Commission – *Shell UK Oil*, HMSO, 1979.
Monopolies Commission – *Starch, Glucoses and Modified Starches*, HMSO, 1971.
Monopolies and Mergers Commission – *Frozen Foodstuffs*, HMSO, 1976.
Price Commission – *Royal Doulton Tableware Ltd – China and Earthenware, Tableware and Ornamental Items*, HMSO, 1978.
Price Commission – *Bass Ltd – Wholesale Prices of Beer and Prices in Managed Houses*, HMSO, 1979.

NON-MARKET LEADERS

Dominant firms

Price Commission – *Rugby Portland Cement Company Ltd – Cements*, HMSO, 1979.
Price Commission – *Air Products Ltd – Merchant Industrial Gases*, HMSO, 1978.

Concentrated oligopoly

Monopolies and Mergers Commission – *Flour and Bread*, HMSO, 1977.
Monopolies and Mergers Commission – *Ice Cream and Water Ices*, HMSO, 1979.
Monopolies Commission – *Household Detergents*, HMSO, 1966.
Monopolies and Mergers Commission – *Electricity Supply Meters*, HMSO, 1979.
Monopolies and Mergers Commission – *Insulated Electric Wires and Cables*, HMSO, 1979.
Monopolies Commission – *Electric Lamps*, HMSO, 1968.
Monopolies and Mergers Commission – *Ceramic Sanitaryware*, HMSO, 1978.
Monopolies and Mergers Commission – *Concrete Roofing Tiles*, HMSO, 1981.
Monopolies and Mergers Commission – *Rockware Group Ltd, United Glass Ltd, Redfearn National Glass Ltd, Report on the Proposed Mergers*, HMSO, 1978.
Monopolies and Mergers Commission – *Cat and Dog Foods*, HMSO, 1977.
Monopolies and Mergers Commission – *Davy International Ltd and The British Rollermakers Corporation Ltd, Report on the Proposed Merger*, HMSO, 1974.
Monopolies and Mergers Commission – *Domestic Gas Appliances*, HMSO, 1980.

Loose oligopoly

Monopolies and Mergers Commission – *Flour and Bread*, HMSO, 1977.
Monopolies and Mergers Commission – *Insulated Electric Wires and Cables*, HMSO, 1979.
Monopolies and Mergers Commission – *Ready Mixed Concrete*, HMSO, 1981.
Price Commission – *BP Oil Ltd – Oil and Petroleum Products*, HMSO, 1979.
Price Commission – *Esso Petroleum Company Ltd – Oil and Petroleum Products*, HMSO, 1979.
Monopolies and Mergers Commission – *Frozen Foodstuffs*, HMSO, 1976.
Price Commission – *Whitbread and Company Ltd – Wholesale Prices and Prices in Managed Houses of Beer, Wines, Spirits, Soft Drinks and Ciders*, HMSO, 1979.
Monopolies and Mergers Commission – *Nabisco Brands Inc and Huntley and Palmers Foods PLC*, Report on the Proposed Merger, HMSO, 1982.

APPENDIX 3.1

MARKET SHARES OF THE DOMINANT FIRM IN SIX UK INDUSTRIES FOR SELECTED DATES

Industry	Firm	Date	Market share (%)
Cement	APCM	1900	59
		1922	75
		1928	58
		1938	70
		1955	67
		1959	*60*
		1968	62
		1973	61
		1978	58
Cigarettes	Imperial	1903	71
		1920	91
		1933	74
		1938	84
		1954	77
		1959	*65*
		1964	56
		1970	67
		1976	66
Flat Glass	Pilkington	1904	29
		1913	36
		1930	37
		1935	58
		1955	*95*
		1967	91
		1980	77
Soap	Lever	1915	46
		1921	67
		1929	60
		1938	52
		1954	52
		1961	*59*
		1976	41

Industry	Firm	Date	Market share (%)
Tyres and tubes	Dunlop	1924	58
		1935	57
		1952	*47*
		1975	27
Cars	Morris-BMC-BL	1924	31
		1929	35
		1938	24
		1952 pre-merger	20
		1952 post-merger	39
		1961	39
		1964	*37*
		1966	39
		1968	45
		1970	48
		1976	28

Source: Stigler (1966) and appendix 3.2.

APPENDIX 3.2

SOURCES USED IN TABLE 3

Matches

Monopolies and Restrictive Practices Commission, Report on the Supply and Export of Matches and the Supply of Match-Making Machinery, HC 161, HMSO, 1953.

Monopolies Commission, Report on the Proposed Merger between British Match Corporation and Wilkinson Sword Ltd, *Cmnd* 5442, HMSO, 1974.

Tyres

Stigler *op. cit.*

Fishwick, F., *Study of the Evolution of Concentration in the UK Manufacture and Supply of Tyres*, EEC Commission, 1977.

Soap

Evely, R. and Little, I. M. D., *Concentration in British Industry*, Cambridge University Press, 1960.

Stigler *op. cit.*

Price Commission, Lever Brothers Ltd – Soaps, Detergents and Related Products, HMSO, 1978.

Price Commission, Proctor and Gamble Ltd – Soaps and Detergents, HMSO, 1978.

Open Top Cans

Monopolies Commission, Report on the Supply of Metal Containers, HMSO, 1970.

Price Commission, Metal Box Ltd – Open Top Food and Beverage and Aerosol Cans, HMSO, 1978.

Industrial Gases

Monopolies and Restrictive Practices Commission, Report on the Supply of Certain Industrial and Medical Gases, HMSO, 1956.

Price Commission, Air Products Ltd – Merchant Industrial Gases, HMSO, 1978.

Price Commission, BOC Ltd – Compressed Permanent Gases and Dissolved Acetylene Sold in Cylinders, Cylinder Rentals and Fixed Charges, HMSO, 1979.

Wallpaper

Monopolies Commission, Report on the Supply of Wallpaper, HMSO, 1964.

Market Intelligence Reports (MINTEL), January 1979.

Retail Business, October 1976.

Cigarettes

Monopolies Commission, Report on the Supply of Cigarettes and Tobacco and of Cigarette and Tobacco Machinery, HMSO, 1961.

Price Commission, Imperial Tobacco Ltd – Cigarettes and Cigarillos, HMSO, 1978.

Asbestos

Monopolies Commission, Asbestos and Certain Asbestos Products, HMSO, 1973.

Evely, R. and Little, I. M. D., *Concentration in British Industry*, Cambridge University Press, 1960.

Petrol

Monopolies Commission, Petrol, HMSO, 1965.

Monopolies and Mergers Commission, Petrol, HMSO, 1979.

Price Commission, Esso Petroleum Co Ltd – Oil and Petroleum Products, HMSO, 1979.

Price Commission, BP Oil Ltd – Oil and Petroleum Products, HMSO, 1979.

Starch

Monopolies Commission, Glucoses and Modified Starches, HMSO, 1971.

Price Commission, CPC (United Kingdom) Ltd – Increases in the prices of Maize Starch, Glucose Syrups, Starch-derived and Glucose-derived Products, HMSO, 1978.

Cement

Stigler, *op. cit.*

Price Commission, Associated Portland Cement Manufacturers Ltd – Increases in Cement Prices, HMSO, 1978.

Price Commission, Rugby Portland Cement Company Ltd – Cements, HMSO, 1979.

Detergents

Monopolies Commission, Household Detergents, HMSO, 1966.

Price Commission, Lever Brothers Ltd – Soaps, Detergents and Related Products, HMSO, 1978.

Price Commission, Proctor and Gamble Ltd – Soaps and Detergents, HMSO, 1978.

Safety Glass

Monopolies Commission, Flat Glass, HMSO, 1968.

Business Monitor, PQ 463, Glass, Third Quarter 1981, HMSO, 1982.

Breakfast Cereal

Monopolies Commission, Breakfast Cereals, HMSO, 1973.

Price Commission, Weetabix Ltd – Cereal and Muesli Products, HMSO, 1978.

Flat glass

As for Safety Glass.

Plasterboard

Bowley, M, *Innovations in Building Materials*, Duckworth, 1960.
Monopolies Commission, Plasterboard, HMSO, 1974.
Price Commission, British Gypsum Ltd – Increases in the Prices of Gypsum-related Products, HMSO, 1978.

Clutches

Monopolies Commission, Clutch Mechanisms for Road Vehicles, HMSO, 1968.
Bhaskar, J., *The Future of the UK Motor Industry*, Kogan Page, 1979.

Cellulosic Fibre

Monopolies Commission, Man-made Cellulosic Fibres, HMSO, 1968.
Utton, M. A. and Morgan, A. D., *Concentration and Foreign Trade*, Cambridge University Press, 1983.

Contraceptives

Monopolies and Mergers Commission, Contraceptive Sheaths, HMSO. 1975.
Monopolies and Mergers Commission, Contraceptive Sheaths, HMSO, 1982.

APPENDIX 4.1

CHANGES IN THE NUMBER OF ENTERPRISES IN CERTAIN PRODUCT GROUPS, 1958–77

In the concentration table for 1977, supplied by the Business Statistics Office, the number of enterprises operating in each product group is given. The comparable data for 1958 were not given in the concentration table published in the summary volume of the 1963 Census of Production. In table 4 of the reports on individual industries in the 1958 Census of Production, however, the sales of principal products and the number of enterprises involved were usually given. In some cases figures were omitted for disclosure reasons and these could not be included in table 4. In other cases the principal products concerned were broken down into finer categories than those shown in the concentration table and it was not possible, therefore, to estimate the precise number of enterprises for the product groups in table 4. It was, however, possible to determine the maximum and minimum number of enterprises in several cases. The maximum number was based on the assumption that firms listed in each sub-category of a principal product made that product only. Hence the maximum number of firms was obtained simply by adding all firms in each sub-category. The minimum number was based on the assumption that the sub-category with the largest number of firms represented the total number of firms producing the principal product. Thus, for example, if a principal product was broken down into three sub-categories with ten, twelve and eighteen firms in them respectively, the maximum number would be forty and the minimum number, eighteen. In four cases the 1977 figure fell between the maximum and minimum values so the direction of change was indeterminate but in the fifteen cases mentioned in table 4 the direction of change was clear. The details are given in the following table together with the adjusted concentration ratios.

Table 4A.1. *Products with adjusted concentration of 75 per cent or above in 1958*

Product	1958	1963	1968	1975	1977	Estimated no. of enterprises in 1958 Min.		Max.	No. of enterprises in 1977
Condensed milk	89.2	89.7	91.1	84.4	83.9	10		18	6
Vegetables, quick frozen	79.9	72.6	79.6	75.1	70.1	9		17	27
Soups	85.4	90.8	88.6	66.8	60.9	34		49	19
Margarine	87.2	91.3	93.5	94.6	93.5	15		28	7
Compound fat	82.5	82.6	81.7	87.9	86.5	17		30	12
Coffee & coffee etc. extracts	88.4	91.7	88.5	80.1	73.2		n.a.		
Blended whisky	96.1	94.2	91.0	86.7	83.8	14		36	24
Alcoholic cider etc.	80.6	97.1	91.0	90.1	92.4		n.a.		
Soap	83.2	80.8	79.5	74.9	75.4		n.a.		71
Fin. organic dyestuffs	87.4	79.4	70.4	70.6	63.3		n.a.		13
Ball & roller bearings & parts	88.4	77.6	79.1	67.8	61.8		36		19
Line apparatus	85.6	94.2	97.3	82.9	92.3		15		12
Valves, cathode ray tubes	82.3	67.6	66.5	53.3	41.0	14		80	25
Gramophone records	97.8	94.6	92.0	68.8	68.1		12		12
Tractors	95.1	97.0	94.1	89.7	87.3		20		11
Cars	89.7	88.6	93.7	72.5	62.6	15		43	19
Commercial vehicles	75.9	84.4	89.9	79.7	77.9		n.a.		44
Motorcycles etc.	75.3	74.2	78.0	48.5	42.4		n.a.		13
Finished thread	84.9	81.4	87.3	86.4	84.3	27	60	1	26
Asbestos manuf.	76.6	81.2	84.2	80.3	81.3		n.a.		18
Electrical ware of porcelain	75.7	78.1	74.4	69.2	70.6		16		17
Illuminating glassware	82.7	79.5	81.6	78.9	75.7	15		43	9
Safety glass	97.6	96.5	95.2	85.9	84.0		22		16
Cement	84.9	87.6	87.4	92.4	92.8	15		32	10
Abrasive wheels etc.	85.6	85.6	85.5	73.2	69.3	12		33	31
Asbestos cement goods	96.5	90.6	92.9	88.2	89.7		n.a.		9
Wallpaper	90.9	91.2	88.5	73.0	72.8	11		16	21
Tyres and tubes	92.3	92.5	84.6	84.2	78.5		n.a.		7

Source: As table 4.1 and Census of Production for 1958, HMSO, 1960–1.

Table 4A.2. *Actual and predicted levels of concentration in several years for 34 heavily concentrated products in 1958, and average concentration for the full sample.*

End year	Five firm mean concentration unadjusted (%)		
	Heavily concentrated products in 1958 (34)		Full sample (119)
	Actual	Predicted	
1958	88.6	—	56.1
1963	89.6	89.8	59.6
1968	90.6	91.9	64.4
1975	87.3	88.2	64.7
1977	86.9	87.5	64.6

Source: Statistics of Product Concentration of UK Manufactures for 1963, 1968 and 1975, Business Monitor PO 1006, HMSO, 1979. *Product Concentration for 1977*, Mimeo, Business Statistics Office, 1981.

NOTES

1 INTRODUCTION

1 For a general treatment of these ideas see Kirzner (1973) and for one written from a British perspective Littlechild (1978).
2 The usual exception mentioned is the grant of a legal monopoly or other impediment to entry backed by the authority of the Government.
3 If they cannot earn a normal return then the industry becomes a natural monopoly.
4 The recent criticism in Geroski and Jacquemin (1984) of the Worcester analysis which merely refers to the short-term price leadership aspect, and *not* to the dominant firm's response is thus largely misplaced.
5 Or, indeed, the expansion of fringe firms at the expense of the leader.
6 This is clearly more probable in cases of acquisition which are open for everyone to see, whereas predatory pricing may remain hidden or disguised for a long period and only emerge after detailed investigation.
7 Both Scherer, for example, and Shepherd, to whose work on market shares we refer below, are agreed that there is quite extensive case material showing that the market share of dominant firms declines over time, see Scherer (1980) pp. 239–42, Shepherd (1975) p. 99 and chapter 3 below.
8 Fisher's article is a very good illustration of the recent reassessment that has been taking place on the whole subject to entry barriers in oligopoly. See also, for example, Demsetz (1982) and Waterson (1981).
9 Part of the slowing down of market share decline after the Second World War may simply be a reflection of the growing maturity of the United States economy compared with the earlier period, the beginning of which came shortly after the first great merger wave in American industry. In view of the much tougher and more effective anti-merger policy after 1950 in the United States, dominant firms had evidently found other ways than acquisition of rivals to slow down the decline of their market share.
10 They included the combined market share of the rest of the leading group, the overall size of firm, firm advertising intensity and the growth of the market. The subsequent studies mentioned have generally included very similar explanatory variables. In some cases interaction terms have been included (for example, market share × product differentiation) with rather mixed results.
11 Except in those relatively few cases where very high market shares are shown to persist.
12 Non primary activities of the firms were excluded in the Shepherd study and weights for the estimated shares were based primarily on measures of sales

and employment levels gathered from various firm and industry sources (Shepherd, 1975, p. 29fn).

2 PROFITABILITY AND MARKET SHARES

1 His empirical work led him to propose a progressive tax based on market share (see Shepherd, 1975, p. 197).

2 The main source was MMC reports but in a number of cases similar information was available from the reports of the Price Commission.

3 It is not really feasible to make direct comparisons between the concentration level in a sample of MMC markets and the published concentration ratios, since the latter refer to the sales of the top five enterprises whereas frequently the MMC only gives market shares for the largest two to four enterprises.

4 A potentially useful source of information on market shares and related variables is the so-called PIMS data (Profit Impact of Marketing Strategies). These have been used fairly extensively in the United States mainly in the business literature. So far similar data for the United Kingdom are not generally available. Since they are collected from firms on a voluntary basis their coverage tends to be rather patchy. More significantly, the method of collection means that data from individual firms cannot be aggregated to form market share profiles in the way that is possible from reports of the Monopolies and Mergers Commission. See, for example, Buzzell *et al.* (1975) and Gale and Branch (1982).

5 We shall see subsequently that there is considerable disagreement both amongst theorists and applied economists as to whether dominant firms actually cede part of their market share in the medium to long term to fringe suppliers and entrants.

6 In the total of 97 market shares used in the sample profits could be averaged over five years in 75 cases. For most of the remainder profits were averaged over three or four years. For full details see appendix 2.1.

7 The calculated value of F was 4.00 and the critical value of F with 2 and 46 degrees of freedom is 3.20 at the 5 per cent level. As noted in the table, three extreme observations were omitted from this calculation. Two cases, LRC and Hoffmann La Roche, had profit relatives of 7.56 and 6.19 respectively which were way above the next closest values. The third case, APCM, managed to earn less than half the manufacturing industry average. Profits in this industry, cement, are still in effect governed by the operations of a cartel, and are exceptionally low. However if all three cases are included in the analysis of variance the result is an estimated F value of 4.81 with a critical value of $F = 3.19$ at the 5 per cent level. The values given in the table, however, seem to reflect more accurately the differences between the groups.

8 An alternative explanation for differential rates of return by dominant firms compared with recent, small entrants is given by Williamson (1977). In his model of strategic investment of dominant firms they can continue to earn super-competitive profits even when entry takes place and prices decline.

9 Although in the two cases mentioned the smaller firms had distinctly higher relative profits than the leading firm – see appendix 2.1.

10 In some cases where information is only given in the MMC report for the leading *two* firms in a market it is possible that the profitability of a smaller firm was higher than those given

11 Ideally we should have a sample of markets drawn from the whole population of manufacturing industry, rather than the more oligopolistic parts of it.

12 Note, whereas the control sample covered three years, most observations in the full sample were averages for five years.

13 With the available data we attempted to extend the analysis by considering the effect of overall size and product differentiation on profitability. However, the results using the control sample were inconclusive. They are given in appendix 2.3.

14 Since we are dealing with narrowly defined markets, the well-known relationship between overall firm size and profit stability does not arise because the main influence there is the dampening effect of diversification on large firms' profits.

3 DOMINANT FIRMS IN THE TWENTIETH CENTURY

1 Shepherd (1975, p. 52) is therefore wrong when he concludes his discussion of the same point by saying that 'to the degree that randomness explains how high market shares arise, it should equally cause them later to fall'.

2 See Prais (1976) for a long-run analysis of the British manufacturing sector.

3 He was writing in 1966 only one year after the Monopolies and Mergers Act made provision for sizeable mergers to be referred to the Monopolies and Mergers Commission.

4 Steel has been omitted from this exercise since re-nationalisation in 1968 removed the industry from the private sector.

5 Lever made a number of important acquisitions in the first decade of the century but there was no simultaneous amalgamation as in the case of Imperial Tobacco or the Associated Portland Cement Company.

6 More detail is given for the period from about 1960 in appendix 3.1 and for earlier years the reader can consult Stigler (1966), table 21.

7 Using the Herfindahl index of concentration, $H = \sum_{i=1}^{n} pi^2$, where $p_1 \ldots p_n$ are the shares of individual firms in the market, then if firms with shares p_1 and p_2 merge the index will rise by $(p_1+p_2)^2-p_1^2-p_2^2 = 2p_1p_2$ (Stigler, 1966, p. 262.) Stigler applies this property to estimate the effect of mergers on concentration in the seven industries and shows (p. 290–1) that in the postwar period they were an unimportant source of concentration increase compared with internal growth. For the industries concerned this remained true for the last twenty years or so when mergers generally were having an important effect on the structure of a number of manufacturing industries.

8 But this decline may be more apparent than real (see p. 49 below).

9 In this comparison profits data were available for only nine of the eleven firms in the first category (tyres and soap were excluded). In the second category LRC Products profits were so extraordinarily high that they were omitted from the calculation.

10 The antitrust suit was filed in 1974 and a settlement was reached in 1982. For a detailed discussion of a variety of issues raised by the case see Evans (1983).

11 On the other hand some indirect evidence from an earlier study tended to support the Demsetz view. In a review of sixteen markets where sales were heavily concentrated and import competition minimal, the Monopolies and Mergers Commission had concluded that their technical and innovative performance was at least satisfactory in about three-quarters of the cases while their profitability (interpreted in an allocative sense) was reasonable in two-thirds of the cases (see Utton and Morgan, 1983, chapter 3).

12 In the case of both Bellrock and the ICI plant which involved substantial increases in the market share of a dominant company, the acquisitions had been given prior clearance by the Board of Trade that no reference to the Monopolies and Mergers Commission would be made (Monopolies Commission, 1974, p. 7).

13 For a critical review of these mergers see Cowling *et al.* (1980), chapters 5 and 10.

14 According to Cowling *et al.* (1980, chapter 10), the continuation of acquisitions by Courtaulds well into the 1970s that are listed on pp. 292–3, demonstrates that the recommendation was not acted on.

15 The Board of Trade was notified of Triplex's intention of bidding for BIG but decided not to refer the bid to the Monopolies and Mergers Commission (Monopolies Commission, 1968a, p. 50fn). BPB's acquisition of ICI's plasterboard capacity was done with the blessing of the Board of Trade.

16 The Monopolies Commission report dated January 1964 was prior to the Monopolies and Mergers Act of 1965 which provided for sizeable mergers to be referred.

17 In this respect its reports contrast sharply with, for example, published data on concentration of sales of particular products which, because of the source from which they are drawn, include exports but do not include imports.

18 The 1980 figures were estimated from Business Monitor (Quarterly Series) PQ 463, third quarter 1981, HMSO, 1982.

19 As we mentioned above, other recommendations referred to monitoring Courtaulds' vertical integration with the clothing and textile industries.

20 Courtaulds also retained its holdings in foreign companies.

21 Estimated from the Overseas Trade Statistics and Trade and Industry. We have focused on cellulosic fibres as this was the basis of the original Monopolies Commission report, but clearly for a number of purposes other manmade and natural fibres are close substitutes. For a discussion of this point see Cowling *et al.* (1980), pp. 84–5.

22 British Match had 57 per cent and the remainder came from a number of other producers, mainly foreign (see Walshe, 1974, p. 102).

23 A conclusion also reached by Walshe, writing in 1973 (*ibid*, p. 102).

24 The reason why the Monopolies Commission did not give the kind of detail that is contained in both its earlier report on the match market and in that for cellulosic fibres was probably because the 1973 report concerned the

proposed conglomerate merger between BMC and Wilkinson Sword where no issue of *additional* horizontal market power was involved.

25 We noted in chapter 2 that the company's relative profits were so high, even for a 'dominant firm' that they tended to distort any statistical analysis and therefore had, for the most part, to be omitted.

26 In this category are cement, cigarettes, industrial gases, open top cans, wallpaper, asbestos, petrol and soap.

4 COMBINED MARKET SHARES AND PRICE COLLUSION

1 The equations in table 4.1 were estimated from $C_{t+1} = a + bC_t$, where C_t and C_{t+1} are product concentration in the opening and closing years respectively. The amount of concentration *change* due to regression can then be estimated from $C_{t+1} - C_t = a + (b-1)C_t + e$.

2 If the analysis is repeated using concentration data unadjusted for imports the results are similar. The details are set out in appendix 4A.2.

3 In 1977 the adjusted concentration ratio for finished thread was less than 1 percentage point lower than in 1958. Details of the sample of 28 products are given in appendix table 4A.1.

4 The concentration table for 1977 was prepared by the Business Statistics Office and used in Utton and Morgan (1983) but was not published.

5 A comparison of the concentration ratios unadjusted for imports, although reducing the *extent* of the decline, does not change the overall picture: for only one product, illuminating glassware, is the direction of change altered from a decrease to an increase and one product, tractors, changes from declining to unchanged concentration.

6 In the case of cement, of course, this is literally true since the Cement Manufacturers' Federation has twice successfully defended the maintenance of their cartel in the Restrictive Practices Court.

5 SUMMARY AND CONCLUSIONS

1 The problem has often been much more acute in horizontal merger cases where the effect on 'market' share may be crucial to the eventual recommendations, see Rowley (1968).

2 For details of this and other proposals see Scherer (1980), pp. 540–2.

3 The Green Paper entitled: A Review of Monopolies and Mergers Policy HMSO (1978).

4 The *Observer* alleged that officials in the National Health Service had 'colluded' to help maintain LRC's monopoly position.

APPENDIX 2.3

1 In markets where they are attempting to gain a foothold it is frequently alleged that such firms engage in cross-subsidisation and even predatory pricing, although the evidence on this is unconvincing (see, for example, Utton, 1979).

2 The multiple regression results (with 40 observations, since two firms were not included as they were foreign owned and a group net asset figure was not available) were as follows, with relative profitability as the dependent variable:

Constant	Market share	Overall size	Product differentiation	R^2
0.525	0.029*	−0.001	−0.069	0.301
(0.328)	(0.008)	(0.001)	(0.354)	

* Significant at the 1 per cent level.
Standard errors in brackets.

WORKS CITED

Bond, R. S. and Greenberg, W. (1976), 'Industry structure, market rivalry, and public policy: a comment', *Journal of Law and Economics*, vol. XIX(1).

Brozen, Y. (1971), 'The persistence of 'high rates of return' in high–stable concentration industries', *Journal of Law and Economics*, vol. XIV.

(1982), *Concentration, Mergers and Public Policy*, New York, Macmillan.

Business Statistics Office (1979), *Statistics of Product Concentration of UK Manufacturers for 1963, 1968 and 1975*, HMSO.

Buzzell, R. D., Gale, B. T. and Sultan, R. G. M. (1975), 'Market share – a key to profitability', *Harvard Business Review*.

Comanor, W. S. and Wilson, T. A. (1974), *Advertising and Market Power*, Harvard University Press.

Cowling, K. (1982), *Monopoly Capitalism*, Macmillan.

Cowling, K., Stoneman, P., Cubbin, J., Cable, J., Hall, G., Domberger, S. and Dutton, P. (1980), *Mergers and Economic Performance*, Cambridge University Press.

Dalton, J. A. and Levin, S. L. (1977), 'Market power: concentration and market share', *Industrial Organisation Review*.

Demsetz, H. (1973a), 'Industry structure, market rivalry and public policy', *Journal of Law and Economics*.

(1973b), 'Market rivalry, efficiency and economic performance', *Journal of Law and Economics*.

(1982), 'Barriers to entry', *American Economic Review*, vol. 72, no. 1.

Dewey, D. J. (1959), *Monopoly in Economics and Law*, Rand McNally.

Evans, D. S. (ed.) (1983), *Breaking Up Bell*, North-Holland.

Fellner, W. J. (1955), 'Economic Theory and Concentration Measurement', Comment in National Bureau of Economic Research, *Business Concentration and Price Policy*, Princeton University Press.

Fisher, F. M. (1979), 'Diagnosing monopoly', *Quarterly Review of Economics and Business*, vol. 19, no. 2.

Gale, B. T. (1972), 'Market share and rate of return', *Review of Economics and Statistics*, November.

Gale, B. T. and Branch, B. S. (1982), 'Concentration versus market share: which determines performance and why does it matter', *Antitrust Bulletin*, vol. XXVII, no. 1.

Geroski, P. A. and Jacquemin, A. (1984), 'Dominant firms and their alleged decline', *International Journal of Industrial Organisation*, vol. 2.

Hart, P. E. and Clarke, R. (1980), *Concentration in British Industry, 1935–75*, Cambridge University Press.

Hart, P. E., Utton, M. A. and Walshe, G. (1973), *Mergers and Concentration in British Industry*, Cambridge University Press.

Kirzner, I. (1973), *Competition and Entrepreneurship*, University of Chicago Press.

Kwoka, J. E. (1978), *Market Shares, Concentration and Competition in Manufacturing Industries*, Federal Trade Commission, Washington.

(1979), 'The effect of market share distribution on industry performance', *Review of Economics and Statistics*, vol. LXI, no. 1.

Littlechild, S. C. (1978), *The Fallacy of the Mixed Economy*, Institute of Economic Affairs.

(1981), 'Misleading calculations of the social costs of monopoly power', *Economic Journal*, vol. 91, no. 362.

Macavoy, P., McKie, J. W. and Preston, L. E. (1971), 'High and stable concentration levels, profitability and public policy: a response', *Journal of Law and Economics*, vol. XIV.

McGee, J. S. (1981), 'Predatory pricing revisited', *Journal of Law and Economics.*

Monopolies Commission (1968a), *Flat Glass*, HMSO, HC 83.

(1968b), *Man-made Cellulosic Fibres*, HMSO, HC 130.

(1973), *British Match Corporation Ltd and Wilkinson Sword Ltd, Cmnd* 5442, HMSO.

(1974), *Plasterboard*, HMSO, HC 94.

(1975), *Contraceptive Sheaths*, HMSO, HC 135.

Pashigian, B. P. (1968), 'Limit price and the market share of the leading firm', *Journal of Industrial Economics*, July.

Porter, M. E. (1979), 'The structure within industries and companies performance', *Review of Economics and Statistics*, vol. LXI, no. 2.

Posner, R. A. (1976), *Antitrust Law*, University of Chicago Press.

Prais, S. J. (1958), 'The statistical conditions for a change in business concentration', *Review of Economics and Statistics*, August.

(1976), *The Evolution of Giant Firms in Britain*, Cambridge University Press.

Reekie, W. D. (1979), *Industry, Markets and Prices*, Phillip Allan.

Review of Monopolies and Mergers Policy (1978), HMSO.

Rosenbluth, G. (1976), 'Comment' in *Journal of Law and Economics*, vol. XIX(2).

Round, D. K. (1975), 'Industry structure, market rivalry and public policy: some Australian evidence', *Journal of Law and Economics*, April.

Rowley, C. K. (1968), 'Mergers and public policy in Great Britain', *Journal of Law and Economics.*

Scherer, F. M. (1980), *Industrial Market Structure and Economic Performance*, Rand McNally, second edition.

Shepherd, W. G. (1972), 'The elements of market structure', *Review of Economics and Statistics*, February.

(1975), *The Treatment of Market Power*, Columbia University Press.

(1979), *The Economics of Industrial Organisation*, Prentice Hall.

(1982), 'Causes of increased competition in the US economy, 1939–1980', *Review of Economics and Statistics*, vol. LXIV, NO. 4.

(1983), 'Long-run market power of dominant firms in US', *Review of Economics and Statistics.*

Stigler, G. J. (1964), 'A theory of oligopoly', *Journal of Political Economy*, February.

(1965), 'The dominant firm and the inverted umbrella', *Journal of Law and Economics*.
(1966a), *The Theory of Price*, Collier-Macmillan.
(1966b), 'The economic effects of the antitrust laws', *Journal of Law and Economics*.
Utton, M. A. (1979), *Diversification and Competition*, Cambridge University Press.
Utton, M. A. and Morgan, A. D. (1983), *Concentration and Foreign Trade*, Cambridge University Press.
Walshe, G. (1974), *Recent Trends in Monopoly in Great Britain*, Cambridge University Press.
Waterson, M. (1981), 'On the definition and meaning of barriers to entry', The *Antitrust Bulletin*, vol. XXVI, no. 3.
Williamson, O. E. (1972), 'Dominant firms and the monopoly problem: market failure considerations', *Harvard Law Review*.
(1977), 'Predatory pricing: a strategic and welfare analysis', *Yale Law Journal*.
Worcester, D. D. (1957), 'Why 'dominant firms' decline', *Journal of Political Economy*, vol. LXV.

INDEX